RETIREMENT ISSUES, PLANS AND LIFESTYLES

OVERVIEW OF THE EMPLOYEE RETIREMENT INCOME SECURITY ACT (ERISA) - PROTECTING EMPLOYEE BENEFIT PLAN

RETIREMENT ISSUES, PLANS AND LIFESTYLES

Additional books in this series can be found on Nova's website at:

https://www.novapublishers.com/catalog/index.php?cPath=23_29&seriesp=Retirement+Issues%2C+Plans+and+Lifestyles

Additional E-books in this series can be found on Nova's website at:

https://www.novapublishers.com/catalog/index.php?cPath=23_29&seriespe=Retirement+Issues%2C+Plans+and+Lifestyles

RETIREMENT ISSUES, PLANS AND LIFESTYLES

OVERVIEW OF THE EMPLOYEE RETIREMENT INCOME SECURITY ACT (ERISA) - PROTECTING EMPLOYEE BENEFIT PLAN

TERRENCE D. ANDERSON
EDITOR

Nova Science Publishers, Inc.
New York

For permission to use material from this book please contact us:
Telephone 631-231-7269; Fax 631-231-8175
Web Site: http://www.novapublishers.com

LIBRARY OF CONGRESS CATALOGING-IN-PUBLICATION DATA

Overview of the Employee Retirement Income Security Act (ERISA) : protecting employee benefit plan / editor, Terrence D. Anderson.
p. cm.
Includes index.
ISBN 978-1-60741-757-6 (softcover)
1. Pension funds--Law and legislation--United States. I. Anderson, Terrence D.
KF3512.O94 2010
344.7301'2524--dc22

2010012237

Published by Nova Science Publishers, Inc. † New York

CONTENTS

PREFACE

The Employee Retirement Income Security Act of 1974 (ERISA) provides a comprehensive federal scheme for the regulation of employee pension and welfare benefit plans offered by employers. ERISA contains various provisions intended to protect the rights of plan participants and beneficiaries in employee benefit plans. This book provides background on the pension laws prior to ERISA, discusses various types of employee benefit plans governed by ERISA, provides an overview of ERISA's requirements, discusses breach of fiduciary duty claims under ERISA Section 502(a)(2) and the LaRue case and examines the regulation of health benefits under ERISA.

Chapter 1 - In *LaRue v. De Wolff, Boberg & Associates*, a participant in a 401(k) plan requested that plan administrators change an investment in his individual account. The plan administrators failed to make this change, and the individual's account allegedly suffered losses. The participant brought an action against his former employer and the 401(k) plan, claiming the plan administrator breached his fiduciary duty by neglecting to properly follow the investment instructions. At issue in the *LaRue* case was whether an individual could bring an action under ERISA to recover the losses. The Supreme Court held that a plan participant in a 401(k) plan could sue a plan fiduciary under Section 502(a)(2) of ERISA to recover losses caused by a fiduciary breach that only affected his individual account. This chapter discusses breach of fiduciary duty claims under ERISA Section 502(a)(2) and the *LaRue* case, and will be updated as events warrant.

Chapter 2 - The Employee Retirement Income Security Act (ERISA) sets certain federal standards for the provision of health benefits under private-sector, employment-based health plans. These standards regulate the nature and content of health plans and include rules on health care continuation coverage (COBRA), guarantees on the availability and renewability of health care coverage for certain employees and individuals, limitations on exclusions from health care coverage based on preexisting conditions, and parity between medical/surgical benefits and mental health benefits. This chapter discusses certain health benefit requirements under ERISA. It also provides a brief overview of proposed and enacted legislation in the 110th Congress that affects the provision of health benefits, including certain amendments made to ERISA by the Paul Wellstone and Pete Domenici Mental Health Parity and Addiction Equity Act of 2008 (included within P.L. 110-343) and the Genetic Information Nondiscrimination Act of 2008 (P.L. 110-233).

The Employee Retirement Income Security Act of 1974 (ERISA) provides a comprehensive federal scheme for the regulation of private-sector employee benefit plans. While ERISA does not require an employer to offer employee benefits, it does mandate compliance with its provisions if such benefits are offered. Besides the regulation of pension plans, ERISA also regulates welfare benefit plans offered by an employer to provide medical, surgical and other health benefits. ERISA applies to health benefit coverage offered through health insurance or other arrangements (e.g., self-funded plans).

Health plans, like other welfare benefit plans governed by ERISA, must comply with certain standards, including plan fiduciary standards, reporting and disclosure requirements, and procedures for appealing a denied claim for benefits. However, these health plans must also meet additional requirements under ERISA. This chapter discusses some of these additional requirements for health plans, as well as selected proposed and enacted legislation in the 110th Congress that affects the provision of health benefits.

Chapter 3 - The Employee Retirement Income Security Act of 1974 (ERISA) provides a comprehensive federal scheme for the regulation of employee pension and welfare benefit plans offered by employers. ERISA contains various provisions intended to protect the rights of plan participants and beneficiaries in employee benefit plans. These protections include requirements relating to reporting and disclosure, participation, vesting, and benefit accrual, as well as plan funding. ERISA also regulates the responsibilities of plan fiduciaries and other issues regarding plan administration. ERISA contains various standards that a plan must meet in order to receive favorable tax treatment, and also governs plan termination. This chapter provides background on the pension laws prior to ERISA, discusses various types of employee benefit plans governed by ERISA, provides an overview of ERISA's requirements, and includes a glossary of commonly used terms.

In: Overview of the Employee Retirement... ISBN: 978-1-60741-757-6
Editors: Terrence D. Anderson

Chapter 1

LIABILITY OF PLAN FIDUCIARIES UNDER ERISA: LARUE V. DEWOLFF, BOBERG & ASSOCIATES

Jennifer Staman

SUMMARY

In *LaRue v. De Wolff, Boberg & Associates*, a participant in a 401(k) plan requested that plan administrators change an investment in his individual account. The plan administrators failed to make this change, and the individual's account allegedly suffered losses. The participant brought an action against his former employer and the 401(k) plan, claiming the plan administrator breached his fiduciary duty by neglecting to properly follow the investment instructions. At issue in the *LaRue* case was whether an individual could bring an action under ERISA to recover the losses. The Supreme Court held that a plan participant in a 401(k) plan could sue a plan fiduciary under Section 502(a)(2) of ERISA to recover losses caused by a fiduciary breach that only affected his individual account. This chapter discusses breach of fiduciary duty claims under ERISA Section 502(a)(2) and the *LaRue* case, and will be updated as events warrant.

BACKGROUND

The Employee Retirement Income Security Act of 1974 (ERISA)[1] provides a comprehensive federal scheme for the regulation of private-sector employee benefit plans. One of the primary goals in enacting ERISA was to "protect ... the interests of participants and ... beneficiaries" of employee benefit plans, and assure that participants receive promised benefits from their employers.[2] To this end, ERISA "provid[es] for appropriate remedies, sanctions, and ready access to the Federal courts."[3] An integral part of ERISA's enforcement scheme is ERISA Section 502(a), which allows private parties as well as government entities to bring various civil actions to enforce provisions of ERISA.[4]

In general, ERISA regulates two types of pension plans, defined benefit plans and defined contribution plans.[5] A defined benefit plan is a plan under which an employee is promised a specified future benefit, traditionally an annuity beginning at retirement. In a defined benefit plan, the employer bears the investment risk and is responsible for any shortfalls.[6] By contrast, a defined contribution plan provides each participant with an individual account that accrues benefits based on amounts contributed to the account by both the employer and the employee.[7] The employee bears the investment risk, and thus the value of the account at the time of retirement is unknown. ERISA subjects both defined benefit and defined contribution plans to a number of requirements, including requirements for fiduciary responsibility.[8]

Claims to Redress Breaches of Fiduciary Duty

Section 502(a)(2) of ERISA authorizes the Secretary of Labor, a participant, a beneficiary, or a plan fiduciary to bring a civil action caused by a breach of fiduciary duty under Section 409 of ERISA. That section makes a plan fiduciary personally liable for breaches against an ERISA plan, and a breaching fiduciary must make good to the plan "any losses to the plan resulting from a breach" and restore to the plan any profits made from using the assets of the plan in improper ways.[9] It also subjects such a fiduciary to other relief as a court may deem appropriate, including removal of the fiduciary.

One controversial issue with respect to breach of fiduciary duty claims under ERISA is that while an individual plaintiff (*e.g.*, a plan participant) may bring a civil action under Section 502(a)(2), the Supreme Court has found that any recovery must "inure[] to the benefit of a plan as a whole."[10] In *Massachusetts Mutual Life Insurance Co. v. Russell*,[11] the Supreme Court ruled that a plan beneficiary could not bring a civil action for monetary damages against a plan fiduciary who had been responsible for the improper processing of a benefit claim. The plaintiff in *Russell*, who was disabled with a back ailment, alleged that she was injured when her employer's disability committee terminated her disability benefits. The Court rejected the beneficiary's claim, explaining ERISA Section 409 did not authorize a beneficiary to bring a claim against a fiduciary for monetary damages. Based on the text of Section 409 and the legislative history of ERISA, the Court opined that relief for an individual beneficiary was not available under Section 409 based on the idea that a plaintiff could only recover losses on behalf of the entire plan.

LaRue v. DeWolff, Boberg & Associates

In *LaRue*, the plaintiff, a participant in a 401(k) plan administered by his former employer, requested that plan administrators change an investment in his individual account. The plan administrators failed to make this change, and the individual's account allegedly suffered losses of approximately $150,000. LaRue brought an action against his former employer and the 401(k) plan, claiming the plan administrator breached his fiduciary duty by neglecting to properly follow the investment instructions.

LaRue brought a claim in district court under ERISA Section 502(a)(3), which permits a participant to bring a civil action to enjoin any act or practice which violates ERISA or the terms of the plan, or obtain "appropriate equitable relief" for these violations.[12] The participant argued that because the defendants failed to invest the money as he directed, his account was depleted and he was entitled to receive "make-whole" or "other equitable relief" under Section 502(a)(3).[13] The district court dismissed the participant's claims, holding that because the defendant did not possess any of the funds belonging to the participant, the relief the participant sought was monetary damages, and this remedy was not available to the plaintiff as "equitable relief" under Section 502(a)(3).

LaRue appealed the decision, arguing to the Fourth Circuit Court of Appeals that he should be able to recoup losses under both 502(a)(3) and

502(a)(2) of ERISA.[14] The court affirmed the district court's decision with regard to Section 502(a)(3), finding that the make-whole relief the participant sought could not be characterized as "equitable" relief. With regard to Section 502(a)(2), the court found that because the argument regarding Section 502(a)(2) was raised for the first time on appeal, the argument was waived. However, the court did discuss the merits of the Section 502(a)(2) claim. Relying on the *Russell* case, the Fourth Circuit held that LaRue's claim failed because Section 502(a)(2) provides remedies only for an entire plan, not for an individual's account. The court focused on the idea that the loss was personal to the defendant and was suffered by him alone. While the court acknowledged that the participant's plan account was indeed part of the "entire plan," the court found no basis to interpret the statute in this manner, and claimed that such an interpretation could undermine Congress's intent to limit the scope of relief under ERISA. Given that the plaintiff sought to recover losses only for himself, the participant could not sue under Section 502(a)(2).

The Supreme Court rejected the Fourth Circuit's decision with respect to Section 502(a)(2), finding that "although §502(a)(2) does not provide a remedy for individual injuries distinct from plan injuries, that provision does authorize recovery for fiduciary breaches that impair the value of plan assets in a participant's individual account."[15] The Department of Labor, writing an amicus brief in *LaRue*, had argued for this result.[16] In explaining the holding, Justice Stevens, writing for the majority, distinguished *LaRue* from the *Russell* case in two ways. First, the Court explained that the type of fiduciary misconduct occurring in *LaRue* violated "principal statutory duties" imposed by ERISA that "relate to the proper plan management, administration, and investment of fund assets."[17] Conversely, in *Russell*, the fiduciary's breach (*i.e.*, a delay in processing a benefit claim) fell outside of these principal duties.[18]

Second, the Court found that in *Russell,* the emphasis placed on protecting the "entire plan" from fiduciary breach under Section 409 applies to defined benefit plans, which were the norm at the time of the case.[19] However, as the Supreme Court noted in *LaRue*, defined contribution plans are more popular today, and the "entire plan" language in *Russell* does not apply to these plans. The Court explained that for defined benefit plans, fiduciary misconduct would not affect an individual entitlement to a benefit unless the misconduct detrimentally affected the entire plan. By contrast, "for defined contribution plans ... fiduciary misconduct need not threaten the solvency of the entire plan to reduce benefits below the amount that participants would otherwise receive."[20] The Court went on to note that "whether a fiduciary breach diminishes plan assets payable to all participants and beneficiaries, or only to persons tied to particular individual accounts, it creates the kinds of harms that concerned the draftsmen of §409."[21]

Although all of the justices agreed on the outcome of the *LaRue* case, they disagreed as to the reasoning behind it. Chief Justice Roberts, joined by Justice Kennedy, wrote a concurring opinion suggesting that it is "at least arguable" that a claim such as the one made in *LaRue* should be evaluated not as a breach of fiduciary duty claim, but as a claim for benefits brought under Section 502(a)(1)(B) of ERISA.[22] Justice Roberts pointed to the fact that allowing a Section 502(a)(1)(B) action to be brought as a claim under Section 502(a)(2) could allow plaintiffs to circumvent certain protections that exist for plan administrators under Section 502(a)(1)(B). For example, as Justice Roberts pointed out, most courts recognize that before a plaintiff can bring a claim for benefits under Section 502(a)(1)(B), that a plaintiff has to exhaust the administrative remedies available under the plan before filing suit. The extra protections for a plan and its administrators, Justice Roberts explains, encourage employers and others to offer benefits to employees.

Justice Thomas, writing a separate concurrence joined by Justice Scalia, found the majority's reliance on "trends in the pension market" and the "concerns of ERISA's drafters" to be misplaced.[23] Justice Thomas concluded that the participant had a legitimate claim based on the "unambiguous text" of Sections 409 and 502(a)(2).[24] Justice Thomas articulated that losses to the participant's individual 401(k) account were losses to the plan, because assets in the participant's account were plan assets. A defined contribution plan, the Justice points out, is not a "collection of unrelated accounts."[25] These plans are "essentially the sum of [their] parts" and that losses to an individual account must be losses to the plan under ERISA.[26]

Concluding Observations

As has been pointed out, the *LaRue* case affirmed that individuals participating in defined contribution plans may bring a claim in the event that a plan fiduciary's inappropriate actions create losses to an individual's account.[27] While some commentators praised the *LaRue* decision for offering protection to individuals in 401(k) plans, others have suggested that the case will likely lead to an increase in litigation of claims by 401(k) participants who have suffered individual account losses.[28] One question arising from the *LaRue* decision is the implications of Justice Roberts's concurrence. Courts may be faced with the issue of whether the availability of relief under Section 502(a)(1)(B) affects a participant's ability to bring a claim under Section 502(a)(2).[29] Another question is whether, under Section 502(a)(2), a participant is required to exhaust administrative remedies provided by a plan before filing suit. This question was raised in a footnote in the majority opinion, but was not answered by the Court.[30]

End Notes

[1] P.L. 93-406, 88 Stat. 829, (Sept. 2, 1974).

[2] See ERISA § 2; 29 U.S.C. § 1001.

[3] ERISA § 2(b); 29 U.S.C. § 1001(b). *See also Aetna Health Inc. v. Davila*, 542 U.S. 200, 208 (U.S. 2004).

[4] 29 U.S.C. § 1132(a).

[5] While not pertinent to this chapter, it should be noted that ERISA also regulates "employee welfare benefit plans." Welfare benefit plans include health plans, life insurance plans, and plans that provide dependent care assistance, educational assistance, or legal assistance. See 29 U.S.C. § 1002(1).

[6] *See* ERISA § 3(35), 29 U.S.C. § 1002(35).

[7] *See* ERISA § 3(34), 29 U.S.C. § 1002(34).

[8] ERISA § 401 *et. seq.*, 29 U.S.C. § 1101 *et. seq.*

[9] ERISA § 409, 29 U.S.C. § 1109.

[10] *Mass. Mut. Life Ins. Co. v. Russell*, 473 U.S. 134, 140 (1985).

[11] *Id.*

[12] Courts sometimes determine whether the relief a plaintiff seeks is legal or equitable. Colleen Murphy, *Money as a "Specific" Remedy*, 58 Ala. L. Rev. 119, 134 (2006). This distinction dates back to the "days of the divided bench," when England (and subsequently the United States) maintained separate courts of law and courts of equity. *See generally Great-West Life & Annuity Ins. Co. v. Knudson*, 534 U.S. 204, 212 (2002). One important way these courts differed from each other was the remedies available to plaintiffs. Historically, the most common remedy in the courts of law was money. *Id.* at 135. The most common remedy in the courts of equity was an order for an individual to do something or refrain from doing something, such as with an injunction. *Id.* The scope of remedies available at law and at equity have been the subject of debate. While there is no longer this divided court system, courts may still evaluate a claim based on this dichotomy.

[13] *LaRue v. DeWolff, Boberg & Associates*, Civil Action No. 2:04-1747-18 (D.S.C. 2005).

[14] *LaRue v. DeWolff, Boberg & Associates*, 450 F.3d 570 (4th Cir. 2006).

[15] *LaRue v. DeWolff, Boberg & Associates*, 2008 LEXIS 2014 at 14 (2008). The Court declined to address the section 502(a)(3) issue, due to the fact that the Court found that the court of appeals erred in its interpretation of section 502(a)(2). *Id.* at 5.

[16] Brief for the United States as Amicus Curiae, *LaRue v. DeWolff, Boberg & Associates*, 2008 LEXIS 2014 (2008) (No. 06-856).

[17] *Id.* at 9 (*quoting Russell*, 473 U.S. at 142).

[18] In addition, as the Court points out, unlike *LaRue*, the plaintiff in *Russell* received all the benefits to which she was entitled. 2008 LEXIS 2014 at 10 (2008).

[19] It is important to note that while the plan at issue in *Russell* was a disability plan rather than a defined benefit plan, the Court applied the logic in *Russell* to defined benefit plans. *See id.* at 12-13.

[20] *Id.* at 12.

[21] *Id.* at 13.

[22] Section 502(a)(1)(B)of ERISA authorizes a plaintiff (*i.e.,* a participant or a beneficiary in an ERISA plan) to bring an action against the plan to recover benefits under the terms of the plan that have been wrongfully denied to a participant.

[23] *Id.* at 22 (Thomas, J. concurring).

[24] *Id.*

[25] 2008 LEXIS 2014 at 24 (2008)(Thomas, J. concurring).

[26] *Id.* at 25.

[27] See Michael R. Triplett and Meredith Z. Maresca, *Unanimous Supreme Court Rules Individual Participant Has Section 502 (a) (2) Remedy*, Pension and Benefits Daily Vol. 8, No. 34 (Feb. 21, 2008).

[28] *Id.*

[29] *LaRue v. DeWolff, Boberg & Assocs.*, 2008 U.S. LEXIS 2014 at 20 (2008)(Roberts, J. concurring).

[30] *LaRue v. DeWolff, Boberg & Assocs.*, 2008 U.S. LEXIS 2014 at 8 n.3 (2008).

In: Overview of the Employee Retirement… ISBN: 978-1-60741-757-6
Editors: Terrence D. Anderson

Chapter 2

REGULATION OF HEALTH BENEFITS UNDER ERISA: AN OUTLINE

Jennifer Staman

SUMMARY

The Employee Retirement Income Security Act (ERISA) sets certain federal standards for the provision of health benefits under private-sector, employment-based health plans. These standards regulate the nature and content of health plans and include rules on health care continuation coverage (COBRA), guarantees on the availability and renewability of health care coverage for certain employees and individuals, limitations on exclusions from health care coverage based on preexisting conditions, and parity between medical/surgical benefits and mental health benefits. This chapter discusses certain health benefit requirements under ERISA. It also provides a brief overview of proposed and enacted legislation in the 110th Congress that affects the provision of health benefits, including certain amendments made to ERISA by the Paul Wellstone and Pete Domenici Mental Health Parity and Addiction Equity Act of 2008 (included within P.L. 110-343) and the Genetic Information Nondiscrimination Act of 2008 (P.L. 110-233).

The Employee Retirement Income Security Act of 1974 (ERISA) provides a comprehensive federal scheme for the regulation of private-sector employee benefit plans. While ERISA does not require an employer to offer employee benefits, it does mandate compliance with its provisions if such benefits are offered. Besides the regulation of pension plans, ERISA also regulates welfare benefit plans[1] offered by an employer to provide medical, surgical and other health benefits. ERISA applies to health benefit coverage offered through health insurance or other arrangements (e.g., self-funded plans).[2]

Health plans, like other welfare benefit plans governed by ERISA, must comply with certain standards, including plan fiduciary standards, reporting and disclosure requirements, and procedures for appealing a denied claim for benefits. However, these health plans must also meet additional requirements under ERISA.[3] This chapter discusses some of these additional requirements for health plans, as well as selected proposed and enacted legislation in the 110th Congress that affects the provision of health benefits.[4]

Current Health Benefit Regulation under ERISA

As enacted in 1974, ERISA's regulation of health plan coverage and benefits was limited. However, beginning in 1986, Congress added to ERISA a number of requirements on the nature and content of health plans, including rules governing health care continuation coverage, limitations on exclusions from coverage based on preexisting conditions, parity between medical/surgical benefits and mental health benefits, and minimum hospital stay requirements for mothers following the birth of a child.[5]

COBRA: Continuing Health Care Coverage

The Consolidated Omnibus Budget Reconciliation Act of 1985 (COBRA) added a new Part 6 to Title I of ERISA, which requires the sponsor of a group health plan to provide an option of temporarily continuing health care coverage for plan participants and beneficiaries under certain circumstances.[6] Under ERISA section 601, a plan maintained by an employer with 20 or more employees must provide "qualified beneficiaries"[7] with the option of continuing coverage under the employer's group health plan in the case of certain "qualified events." A qualifying event is an event that, except for continuation coverage under COBRA, would result in a loss of coverage, such as the death of the covered employee, the termination (other than by reason of the employee's gross misconduct) or reduction of hours of the covered employee's employment, or the covered employee becoming entitled to Medicare benefits.[8]

Under section 602 of ERISA, the employer must typically provide this continuation coverage for 18 months.[9] However, coverage may be longer, depending on the qualifying event.[10] Under ERISA 602(1), the benefits offered under COBRA must be identical to the health benefits offered to "similarly situated non-COBRA beneficiaries," or in other words, beneficiaries who have not experienced a qualifying event. The health plan may charge a premium to COBRA participants, but it cannot exceed 102% of the plan's group rate. After 18 months of required coverage, a plan may charge certain participants 150% of the plan's group rate.

Additional Coverage and Benefit Requirements

The Health Insurance Portability and Accountability Act of 1996 (HIPAA) added a new Part 7 to Title I of ERISA to provide additional health plan coverage requirements.[11] Other federal legislation amended Part 7 of ERISA to require plans to offer specific health benefits. The requirements of Part 7 generally apply to group health plans, as well as health insurance issuers that offer group health insurance coverage.[12]

HIPAA

HIPAA amended ERISA to limit the circumstances under which a health plan may exclude a participant or beneficiary with a preexisting condition from coverage.[13] This exclusion from coverage cannot be for more than 12 months after an employee enrolls in a health plan (or 18 months for late enrollees). HIPAA prohibits pre-existing condition coverage exclusions for any conditions relating to pregnancy. Similarly, newborns and adopted children may not be excluded from plan enrollment if they were covered under "creditable coverage" within 30 days after birth or adoption, and there has not been a gap of more than 64 days in this coverage.[14]

HIPAA also created ERISA section 702, which provides that a group health plan or health insurance issuer may not base coverage[15] eligibility rules on certain health-related factors, such as medical history or disability.[16] In addition, a health plan may not require an individual to pay a higher premium or contribution than another "similarly situated" participant, based on these health-related factors.[17] HIPAA also added section 703 of ERISA, which provides that certain health plans covering multiple employers cannot deny an employer (whose employees are covered by the plan) coverage under the plan, except for certain reasons, such as an employer's failure to pay plan contributions.

Mental Health Parity

In 1996, Congress enacted the Mental Health Parity Act (MHPA), which added section 712 of ERISA to create certain requirements for mental health coverage, if this coverage was offered by a health plan.[18] Under the MHPA, health plans are not required to offer mental health benefits. However, plans that choose to provide mental health benefits must not impose lower annual and lifetime dollar limits on these benefits than the limits placed on medical and surgical benefits. The MHPA allows a plan to decide what mental health benefits are to be offered; however, the parity requirements do not apply to substance abuse or chemical dependency treatment.[19]

Certain plans may be exempt from the MHPA. Plans covering employers with 50 or fewer employees are exempt from compliance. In addition, employers that experience an increase in claims costs of at least 1% as a result of MHPA compliance can apply for an exemption. Recently, Congress enacted legislation which expands the MHPA's requirements.[20] The new requirements apply to group health plans for plan years beginning after October 3, 2009.

Maternity Length of Stay

In 1996, Congress passed the Newborns' and Mothers' Health Protection Act (NMHPA), which amended ERISA and established minimum hospital stay requirements for mothers following the birth of a child.[21] In general, the NMHPA prohibits a group health plan or health insurance issuer from limiting a hospital length of stay in connection with childbirth for the mother or newborn child to less than 48 hours, following a normal vaginal delivery, and to less than 96 hours, following a cesarean section.

Reconstructive Surgery Following Mastectomies

The Women's Health and Cancer Rights Act, enacted in 1998, amended ERISA to require group health plans providing mastectomy coverage to cover prosthetic devices and reconstructive surgery.[22] Under section 713 of ERISA, this coverage must be provided in a manner determined in consultation between the attending physician and the patient.[23]

SELECTED LEGISLATION IN THE 110TH CONGRESS

Legislation affecting the provision of health benefits under ERISA was proposed and enacted during the 110th Congress. The legislation included the following:

Enacted Legislation

The Genetic Information Nondiscrimination Act (GINA)

H.R. 493, enacted as P.L. 110-233, amends section 702 of ERISA and prevents a health plan from adjusting premiums or contribution amounts for a group covered by the plan on the basis of genetic information.[24] "Genetic information," as defined by the bill, includes information about a genetic test of an individual or a family member of an individual, the manifestation of a disease or disorder in the family members of an individual, as well as request for, or receipt of, genetic services.[25] GINA restricts a health plan from requiring or requesting an individual or a family member of an individual to undergo a genetic test. The act includes an exception to this provision, under which a health plan may request a genetic test for research purposes, but only if certain conditions are met. Further, GINA prohibits a plan from requesting, requiring, or purchasing genetic information for underwriting purposes[26] or with respect to an individual prior to the individual's enrollment in the plan.

GNA also amends section 502 of ERISA to authorize the Secretary of Labor to impose a penalty of $100 per day (per participant or beneficiary) against a plan that fails to comply with various requirements of the act. Additional penalty amounts may be imposed if the violation is not corrected before a plan receives notice from the Secretary of the violation. The act also contains certain penalty limitations, and provides that in certain cases, the Secretary may waive part or all of the penalty to the extent that the payment of the penalty would be excessive relative to the violation. The amendments made by GINA apply to health plans for plan years beginning after May 21, 2009.

The Paul Wellstone and Pete Domenici Mental Health Parity and Addiction Equity Act of 2008

This act, included as part of the Emergency Economic Stabilization Act of 2008,[27] expands the parity requirements under the current version of the MHPA for mental health and substance use disorder coverage[28] if such coverage is offered by a group health plan. In general, the act amends section 712 of ERISA, as well as other federal laws, to require parity between mental health/substance use disorder benefits and medical/surgical benefits in terms of the predominant (1) financial requirements and (2) treatment limitations imposed by a group health plan. As defined by the act, financial requirements include requirements such as deductibles, co-payments, co-insurance and out-of-pocket expenses; treatment limitations include limits on the frequency of treatment, number of visits, days of coverage, or any other limits on the duration or scope of treatment. The parity requirements of the act apply to mental health and substance use disorder benefits as defined by the health plan or applicable state law. Health plans may qualify for an exemption from the parity requirements if it is actuarially determined that the implementation of the act's requirements would cause a plan to experience an increase in actual total costs of coverage that exceed 2% of the actual total plan costs during the first plan year, or exceed 1% of the actual total plan costs each subsequent year.

Proposed Legislation

The Breast Cancer Patient Protection Act

This legislation (H.R. 758 as passed by the House, H.R. 119, and S. 459) would have amended ERISA and other federal laws to require coverage and radiation therapy for breast cancer treatment. The bills would have prevented the restriction of benefits for any hospital length of stay to less than 48 hours in connection with a mastectomy or breast-conserving surgery, or less than 24 hours in connection with a lymph node dissection, for the treatment of breast cancer.[29] Under the bills, a health plan could not have required a health care provider to obtain authorization from a health plan for prescribing any length of stay required under the act. The bills also stated that a health plan must ensure coverage for secondary consultations by specialists in certain medical fields to confirm or refute an initial diagnosis of cancer.

Access to Cancer Clinical Trials Act of 2008

S. 2999 would have amended ERISA, the Public Health Service Act, and the Internal Revenue Code to provide that if a group health plan provides coverage to a "qualified individual," the plan cannot (1) deny the individual participation in certain clinical trials; (2) deny, limit, or impose additional conditions on coverage of routine patient costs for items or services furnished in connection with trial participation; and (3) may not discriminate against the individual based on trial participation. "Qualified individuals" included individuals diagnosed with cancer and who are eligible to participate in the trial according to the trial protocol. The bill would have applied to clinical trials (*i.e.*, a research studies or clinical investigations) that relate to the treatment of cancer and that are either funded by certain federal agencies, or are part of a drug trial, under certain circumstances.

This chapter will be updated to reflect legislation introduced in the 111th Congress.

End Notes

[1] ERISA considers a number of non-pension benefit programs offered by an employer to be "employee welfare benefit plans." For example, health plans, life insurance plans, and plans that provide dependent care assistance, educational assistance, or legal assistance can all be deemed welfare benefit plans. See 29 U.S.C. § 1002(1).

[2] The regulation of employment-based health benefits is affected by the express preemption provision of ERISA. Section 514(a) ERISA preempts state laws that "relate to" an employee benefit plan. 29 U.S.C. § 1144(a). However, ERISA sets out certain exceptions to the preemption provision, including an exemption for state laws that regulate insurance. 29 U.S.C. § 1144(b). Thus, health benefits offered through health insurance (i.e., where an employer pays a premium to an insurer to cover the claims of plan participants) may be subject to state regulation. Self-funded (or self- insured) plans, under which an employer provides health benefits directly to plan participants, are not exempt from ERISA's preemption provisions and are, therefore, not subject to state law.

[3] See Title I, Part 6 and Part 7 of ERISA, and discussion *infra.*

[4] Other federal laws regulate the provision of health benefits. These laws include the Internal Revenue Code (26 U.S.C. §§ 1 et. seq.), the Public Health Services Act (42 U.S.C. §§ 201 et. seq.), and Medicare (Social Security Act, Title XVIII, 42 U.S.C. §§ 1395 et. seq.). This report addresses only regulation of health benefits under ERISA.

[5] *See generally* Employee Benefits Law 355 (Steven J. Sacher et al., eds., 2000).

[6] P.L. 99-272, tit. X, 100 Stat. 327 (1985). For additional information on COBRA, see CRS Report R40142, *Health Insurance Continuation Coverage Under COBRA*, by Janet Kinzer.

[7] A "qualified beneficiary" can be an employee (who loses health coverage due to termination of employment or a reduction in hours), as well as a spouse or the dependent child of the employee. 29 U.S.C. § 1167.

[8] 29 U.S.C. § 1163.

[9] 29 U.S.C. § 1162(2).

[10] See 29 U.S.C. § 1162(2)(A)(iv). For example, in the case of a death of a covered employee (a qualifying event under section 603(1) of ERISA) coverage can be up to 36 months.

[11] P.L. 104-191, 110 Stat. 1936 (1996). For additional information on HIPAA, see CRS Report RL31634, *The Health Insurance Portability and Accountability Act (HIPAA) of 1996: Overview and Guidance on Frequently Asked Questions*, by Hinda Chaikind et al.

[12] Group health plans and health insurance issuers that provide health coverage will be referred to collectively hereinafter as "health plans."

[13] 29 U.S.C. § 1181(a)(1)-(3).

[14] 29 U.S.C § 1181(d).

[15] "Creditable coverage" as defined under ERISA section 701(c)(1) (29 U.S.C. § 1181(c)(1)) includes coverage under a group health plan, health insurance, and various other means of health benefit coverage.

[16] 29 U.S.C. § 1182(a)(1)(A)-(H).

[17] 29 U.S.C. § 1182(b)(1).

[18] P.L. 104-204, tit.VII, 110 Stat. 2874 (1996).

[19] 29 U.S.C. § 1185a(a)(4).

[20] See section 512 of P.L. 110-343, 122 Stat. 3765 (Oct. 3, 2008), and see *infra* for a discussion of the new requirements.

[21] P.L. 104-204, tit. VI, 110 Stat. 2935 (1996), codified at 29 U.S.C. § 1185.

[22] P.L. 105-277, 112 Stat. 2681 (1998).

[23] 29 U.S.C. § 1185b.

[24] 29 U.S.C. § 1182(b). Genetic information under GINA also includes information about a fetus carried by a pregnant woman or an embryo that is legally held by the individual or a family member.

[25] "Genetic services," as defined by the act, includes genetic tests, genetic counseling (including obtaining, interpreting or assessing genetic information), or genetic education.

[26] "Underwriting purposes," as defined by the act, includes a determination of eligibility for benefits or coverage, computation of a premium or contribution under the plan, the application of a pre-existing condition exclusion, and other activities relating to the creation, renewal or replacement of a contract for health benefits.

[27] P.L. 110-343, 122 Stat. 3765 (Oct. 3, 2008).

[28] Unlike the original version of the MHPA, the act provides that substance-related disorders are subject to the proposed parity requirements.

[29] The bills provided that these requirements should not have been construed as requiring the provision of inpatient coverage if a shorter hospital stay or outpatient treatment was determined to be medically appropriate.

In: Overview of the Employee Retirement... ISBN: 978-1-60741-757-6
Editors: Terrence D. Anderson

Chapter 3

SUMMARY OF THE EMPLOYEE RETIREMENT INCOME SECURITY ACT (ERISA)

***Patrick Purcell*[1] *and Jennifer Staman*[2]**

[1] Income Security Domestic Social Policy Division

[2]American Law Division

SUMMARY

The Employee Retirement Income Security Act of 1974 (ERISA) provides a comprehensive federal scheme for the regulation of employee pension and welfare benefit plans offered by employers. ERISA contains various provisions intended to protect the rights of plan participants and beneficiaries in employee benefit plans. These protections include requirements relating to reporting and disclosure, participation, vesting, and benefit accrual, as well as plan funding. ERISA also regulates the responsibilities of plan fiduciaries and other issues regarding plan administration. ERISA contains various standards that a plan must meet in order to receive favorable tax treatment, and also governs plan termination. This chapter provides background on the pension laws prior to ERISA, discusses various types of employee benefit plans governed by ERISA, provides an overview of ERISA's requirements, and includes a glossary of commonly used terms.

INTRODUCTION

The *Employee Retirement Income Security Act of 1974* (ERISA)[1] protects the interests of participants and beneficiaries in private-sector employee benefit plans. Governmental plans and church plans generally are not subject to the law. ERISA supersedes state laws relating to employee benefit plans except for certain matters such as state insurance, banking and securities laws, and divorce property settlement orders by state courts. An employee benefit plan may be either a pension plan (which provides retirement benefits) or a welfare benefit plan[2] (which provides other kinds of employee benefits such as health and disability benefits). Most ERISA provisions deal with pension plans. ERISA does not require employers to provide pensions or welfare benefit plans, but those that do must comply with its requirements. ERISA sets standards that pension plans must meet in regard to:

who must be covered (participation),
how long a person has to work to be entitled to a pension (vesting), and
how much must be set aside each year to pay future pensions (funding).

ERISA sets fiduciary standards that require employee benefit plan funds be handled prudently and in the best interests of the participants. It requires plans to inform participants of their rights under the plan and of the plan's financial status, and it gives plan participants the right to sue in federal court to recover benefits that they have earned under the plan. ERISA also established the Pension Benefit Guaranty Corporation (PBGC) to insure that plan participants receive promised benefits, up to a statutory limit, should a plan terminate with a lack of sufficient assets to pay promised benefits. In order to encourage employers to establish pension plans, Congress has granted certain tax deductions and deferrals to qualified plans. To be qualified for tax preferences under the Internal Revenue Code (IRC), plans must meet requirements with respect to pension plan contributions, benefits, and distributions, and there are special rules for plans that primarily benefit highly compensated employees or business owners.

Responsibility for enforcing ERISA is shared by the Department of the Treasury, the Department of Labor, and the Pension Benefit Guaranty Corporation (PBGC). In the Department of the Treasury, the Internal Revenue Service oversees standards for plan participation, vesting, and funding. The Department of Labor regulates fiduciary standards and requirements for reporting and disclosure of financial information. The PBGC — a government-owned corporation — administers the pension benefit insurance program.

Historical Development of Pension Plans in the Unites States

The first employer-sponsored pension plans in the United States were established in the late 19th century in the railroad industry. At that time, pensions were regarded as gifts in recognition of long service rather than as a form of compensation protected by law. Pension benefits often were paid from employers' annual revenues and sometimes were reduced or terminated if the company paying the pension became unprofitable or went out of business.

Congress first gave pensions and profit-sharing plans preferential income tax treatment in the 1 920s. At that time, few households paid income taxes, so these tax benefits did not immediately spur the growth of the private pension system. The Revenue Acts of 1938 and 1942 outlined more specific requirements for "tax-qualified" pension plans, including the requirement that benefits and contributions not discriminate in favor of highly compensated employees. Tax qualification means that the employer can deduct the amounts contributed to the plan, the earnings on the pension trust fund are exempt from taxes until distributed, and covered employees do not have to pay income tax on the employer's contributions to the plan.[3] Employers also are allowed to "integrate" their pension benefit formulas with Social Security benefits to partly offset the relatively more generous income replacement rates that Social Security pays to low-wage workers.[4]

During the Second World War (1941-1945), pensions and other deferred compensation arrangements were exempt from wartime wage controls. Employers who were unable to pay higher wages due to these controls could increase workers' total compensation by offering new or increased pension benefits. Also in 1940s, the federal courts declared that pensions were subject to collective bargaining, and that employers had to include pensions among the benefits for which unions could negotiate.[5] In addition, the expansion of the income tax to include more households and the introduction of higher marginal income tax rates made the tax advantages of pensions considerably more valuable to workers. Both of these developments led to more widespread adoption of employer-sponsored pensions during the 1950s and 1960s.

Origins of ERISA

As the number and size of private pension plans grew in the 1950s and 1960s, so did the number of instances in which employers or unions attempted to use the assets of these plans for purposes other than paying benefits to retired workers and their surviving dependents. In 1958, Congress passed *The Welfare and Pension Plans Disclosure Act*,[6] which required public disclosure of pension plan finances. Advocates of the legislation expected that greater transparency of pension funding would ensure that the funds held in trust for workers' pensions would not be misused by plan sponsors. After the Studebaker automobile company terminated its underfunded pension plan in 1963, leaving several thousand workers and retirees without the pensions that they had been promised, Congress began considering legislation to ensure the security of pension benefits in the private sector.

During the early 1970s, both the House and Senate labor committees drafted bills to regulate the private pension system. The Senate Labor and Public Welfare Committee reported a pension bill in 1972. Up to that point, the legislation had been handled exclusively as a labor issue, but since most private pension plans benefitted from the favorable tax treatment accorded them under the Internal Revenue Code, the Senate Finance Committee also asserted its jurisdiction. As passed by Congress in 1974, ERISA included elements produced by the House and Senate labor committees, the House Ways and Means Committee, and the Senate Finance Committee. Title I of the law, which sets standards for pension plans of employers engaged in interstate commerce, is under the jurisdiction of the House Committee on Education and Labor and the Senate Committee on Health, Education, Labor, and Pensions. Title II, which makes conforming amendments to the Internal Revenue Code for tax-qualified plans, is under the jurisdiction of the House Ways and Means Committee and the Senate Finance Committee. The labor and tax committees share jurisdiction over the PBGC.

ERISA was signed into law by President Gerald Ford on Labor Day, September 2, 1974. Congress has amended ERISA over the years to provide greater protection to survivors and spouses of pension plan participants, improve pension funding practices, strengthen the finances of the PBGC, alter the limits on tax-deductible pension plan contributions, and to ensure that tax-favored plans are broadly based and do not unduly favor a firm's owners and other highly compensated employees.

Before ERISA was enacted, an employer could terminate an unfunded pension plan without being liable for any additional pension contributions. If there were insufficient assets in the pension plan to pay all claims, participants had no legal recourse to demand that employers use company assets to continue funding the plan. ERISA protects the benefits of participants in most private-sector pension plans by requiring companies with defined benefit pension plans to fully fund the benefits that participants have earned. The law prohibits companies from using pension funds for purposes other than paying pensions and retiree health benefits. It also limits the age and length-of-service requirements that firms can require participants to meet to receive a pension. ERISA also requires all private-sector sponsors of defined benefit pension plans to purchase insurance from the Pension Benefit Guaranty Corporation.

Types of Qualified Retirement Plans

ERISA and the IRC classify employer-sponsored retirement plans as either *defined benefit* (DB) plans or *defined contribution* (DC) plans.[7] A defined benefit plan specifies either the benefit that will be paid to a plan participant or the method of determining the benefit. The plan sponsor's contributions to the plan vary from year to year, depending on the plan's funding requirements. Benefits often are based on average pay and years of service. For example, the benefit might be defined as 1.5% of the average of the employee's highest five years of pay multiplied by his or her number of years of service. This would result in a benefit equal to 45% of a participant's "high-five" average pay after 30 years of service. Some DB plans, particularly plans covering workers who belong to unions, pay a flat benefit per year of service. For example, if the benefit is defined as $30 per month for each year of service, the monthly pension benefit after 30 years of service would be $900.

ERISA requires DB plans to be fully funded. The assets held in the pension trust must be sufficient to pay the benefits that the plan's participants have earned. The employer bears the investment risk for the assets held by the plan. If the assets decrease in value, or if the plan's liabilities increase, the plan sponsor must make additional contributions to the pension trust fund. The assets of qualified DB plans are exempt from creditors' claims if the sponsor is in bankruptcy, and DB plan benefits are insured up to certain limits by the Pension Benefit Guaranty Corporation.

A defined contribution plan is one in which the contributions are specified, but not the benefits. A defined contribution plan (also called "an individual account" plan) is one that provides an individual account for each participant that accrues benefits based solely on the amount contributed to the account and any income, expenses, and investment gains or losses to the account.[8] The employee bears the investment risk in a DC plan, and DC plans are not insured by the PBGC.

When ERISA was enacted in 1974, most employer-sponsored retirement plans were defined benefit plans. The number of defined benefit plans continued to grow until the mid-1980s. The number of DB plans then began to fall while the number of DC plans increased. Analysts have suggested several possible reasons for these trends, including rising global competition that put greater pressure on companies to reduce costs, a more mobile workforce that preferred the portability of benefits earned in DC plans, the higher costs of maintaining DB plans after stronger funding requirements were put into place by ERISA, and the greater attractiveness of DC plans after Section 401(k) of the tax code was added by the *Revenue Act of 1978*.[9] Although the standards established under ERISA have made workers' pensions more secure, some employers — especially small employers — apparently decided that the plan funding requirements of ERISA made DB plans too expensive to maintain. The decline in the number of DB plans since the 1980s has been the result mainly of terminations of small plans. By the late 1990s, defined contribution plans had overtaken defined benefit plans in number of plans, number of participants, and total assets. (**Table 1**.)

Hybrid Plans

In recent years, many employers have converted their traditional DB plans to "hybrid" plans that have characteristics of both defined benefit and defined contribution plans. The most common of these hybrids is the *cash balance plan*. A cash balance plan looks like a defined contribution plan in that the accrued benefit is defined in terms of an account balance. The employer contributes an amount equal to a fixed percentage of pay to the plan and pays interest on the accumulated balance. However, a cash balance plan is not an individual account owned by the participant. Assets are held in a common trust, and each participant's "account balance" is merely a record of his or her accrued benefit. Because plan sponsors are obligated to provide the participants with benefits that are no less than the sum of contributions to the plan plus interest, cash balance plans are considered to be defined benefit plans.[10]

The Revenue Act of 1978 and 401(k) Plans

The most common defined contribution plans are 401(k) plans, named for the section of the IRC added by the *Revenue Act of 1978* under which they were authorized. In 1981, the IRS published regulations for IRC §401(k). Soon after, the first 401(k) plans were established. A 401(k) plan is an "individual account plan."[11] Its defining feature is that the employee, as well as the employer, can make pre-tax contributions to the account. Taxes on these contributions and on investment earnings are deferred until the money is withdrawn. Before Section 401(k) was enacted, DC plans for private-sector employees were funded by employer contributions or by *after-tax* employee contributions.[12] Typically, participants in a 401(k) plan can allocate their account balances among a menu of investment options selected by the employer or by a plan administrator appointed by the employer. The participant's retirement benefit consists of the balance in the account, which is the sum of all the contributions that have been made plus interest, dividends, and capital gains (or losses) minus fees and expenses. Upon separating from the employer, the participant usually has the choice of receiving these funds through a series of withdrawals or as a lump sum. Some 401(k) plans allow participants to purchase a life annuity through an insurance company, but defined contribution plans are not required to offer annuities.[13]

In most 401(k) plans, the employee must elect to have contributions to the plan deducted from his or her pay, decide how much to have deducted, and direct these contributions among the plan's investment options.[14] The employer often contributes either a fixed dollar amount or percentage of pay to the account on behalf of each participant. Employer contributions are sometimes conditioned on the employee also making contributions. In a 401(k) plan, the employer can reduce or suspend its contributions to the plan if business conditions are unfavorable for the firm, or for any other reason. Although 40 1(k) plans are the most numerous DC plans, they are not the only kind of DC plan. (See box below.)

ERISA and the pension provisions of the Internal Revenue Code have been amended several times since ERISA was enacted in 1974. The most significant changes to ERISA since its original passage were enacted in the *Pension Protection Act of 2006* (P.L. 109-280).[15]

Table 1. Number of Plans, Participants, and Assets by Type of Plan, 1975-2004

Year	Defined Benefit Plans			Defined Contributions Plans		
	Plans	Participants (thousands)	Assets (millions)	Plans	Participants (thousands)	Assets (millions)
1975	103,346	33,004	$185,950	207,748	11,507	$74,014
1980	148,096	37,979	401,455	340,805	19,924	162,096
1985	170,172	39,692	826,117	461,963	34,973	426,622
1990	113,062	38,832	961,904	599,245	38,091	712,236
1995	69,492	39,736	1,402,079	623,912	47,716	1,321,657
2000	48,773	41,613	1,986,177	686,878	61,716	2,216,495
2004	47,503	41,707	2,106,325	635,567	64,627	2,587,152

Source: U.S. Department of Labor, *Private Pension Plan Bulletin: Abstract of Form 5500 Annual Reports*, various years.

Note: Includes active participants, vested separated participants, and retired participants.

Principal Types of Defined Contribution Plans

A. Qualified plans under Internal Revenue Code §401(a)
  1. *Money purchase pension plans*
     a. Traditional money purchase plans
     b. Target benefit plans
     c. Thrift plans (other than profit sharing plans)
  2. *Profit sharing plans*
     a. Traditional profit sharing plans
     b. Thrift plans
     c. Cash or deferred arrangements (IRC §401(k))
  3. *Stock bonus plans*
     a. Traditional stock bonus plans
     b. Employee stock ownership plans (ESOPs)
  4. *Voluntary employee contributions under qualified plans*

B. Tax-deferred annuities under IRC §403(b)

C. Deferred compensation plans for state and local governments and tax-exempt organizations under IRC §457
D. Individual retirement accounts (IRAs and Roth IRAs) under IRC §408 and §408A
E. Non-qualified plans (Plans that do not qualify under the Internal Revenue Code)

Source: D. McGill and D. Grubbs, *Fundamentals of Private Pensions*, 6th edition.

ERISA: An Overview

ERISA consists of four titles. Title I sets out specific protections of employee rights in pensions and welfare benefit plans. Title II specifies the requirements for plan qualification under the Internal Revenue Code. Title III assigns responsibilities for administration and enforcement to the Departments of Labor and Treasury. Title IV of ERISA establishes the Pension Benefit Guaranty Corporation.

ERISA Title I. Protection of Employee Benefit Rights

A. Coverage

ERISA covers employee pensions and welfare benefit plans established by employers in the private sector. The law specifically exempts governmental plans and church plans.[16]

B. Reporting and Disclosure

Section 2(b) of ERISA states that it is the policy of ERISA "to protect ... the interests of plan participants and their beneficiaries by requiring disclosure and reporting of financial and other information." Both pension and welfare benefit plans can be subject to extensive reporting and disclosure requirements that can be found under Sections 101 through 111 of ERISA.[17] These sections may require disclosure of information to plan participants and beneficiaries, as well as reporting of pension and welfare plan information to governmental agencies. Some of the reporting and disclosure requirements provide that certain materials must be disseminated or made available to participants at reasonable times and places. Other requirements arise only upon the written request of a plan participant or beneficiary or upon the occurrence of a specific event. Reports and disclosures required by ERISA include summary plan descriptions, annual reports, and summaries of plan modifications. In addition, the *Pension Protection Act of 2006* (PPA)[18] made enhancements to the reporting and disclosure requirements, requiring the provision of statements of a participant's total accrued benefits,[19] an annual funding notice for single-employer plans, as well as a notice of eligibility to divest employer securities.

1. Summary Plan Description

As a mechanism for informing plan participants of the terms of the plan and its benefits, ERISA requires that plan administrators furnish to participants a summary plan description (SPD).[20] A SPD is a written summary of the provisions of an employee benefit plan that contains the terms of the plan and the benefits offered.[21] It must be written in a manner that can be understood by the average plan participant and be sufficiently accurate and comprehensive to reasonably apprise participants and beneficiaries of their rights and obligations under the plan.[22]

ERISA specifies what the SPD must contain.[23] It must state when an employee can begin to participate in the plan, describe the benefits provided by the plan, state when benefits become vested, and describe the remedies available if a claim for benefits is denied in whole or in part. If a plan is altered, participants must be informed, either through a revised SPD, or in a separate document, called a summary of material modifications (discussed below), both of which must also be given to plan participants.

2. Summary of Material Modifications

Under Section 104(b)(1), a plan administrator must provide a summary of any material modification (SMM) in the terms of the plan as well as any change in information required to be included in the SPD.[24] This summary must be provided, in most cases, within 210 days after the close of the plan year in which the modification was adopted, and also must be furnished to the Labor Department upon request.[25] Similar to the SPD, the materials must be written in a manner that can be understood by the average plan participant. While ERISA does not define "material modification" and does not specifically cover what changes warrant an SMM,[26] courts have addressed this issue.[27] Courts have held plan amendments such as the establishment and elimination of benefits are material modifications.[28] However, as courts have also pointed out, not all plan amendments are material modifications.[29]

3. Annual Report

Section 103 of ERISA provides that certain employee benefit plans must file an annual report with the Department of Labor.[30] The annual report is considered to be a primary source of information concerning the operation, funding, assets, and investments of employee benefit plans.[31] It is regarded as a compliance and research tool for the Labor Department, and a source of information and data for use by other federal agencies, Congress, and private groups in assessing employee benefit, tax, and economic trends and policies.[32] While the annual report can also be an important disclosure document for plan participants, participants must request a copy from a plan administrator.[33]

The annual report must include a detailed financial statement containing information on the plan's assets and liabilities, an actuarial statement, as well as various other information, depending on the type of the plan and the number of participants. Plan administrators must make copies of the annual report available at the principal office of the plan administrator and at other places as may be necessary to make pertinent information readily available to plan participants.[34]

The annual report must be filed within seven months after the close of a plan year, and extensions may be available under certain circumstances.[35] The annual report is to be filed with the Department of Labor on Form 5500.[36] In 2006, the DOL published a rule requiring electronic filing of Form 5500 annual reports for plan years beginning on or after January 1, 2008.[37]

4. Benefit Statements

Under Section 105 of ERISA, plan administrators are required to periodically furnish a pension benefit statement to participants and beneficiaries.[38] For defined contribution plans, a pension benefit statement must be provided (1) every calendar quarter to participants and beneficiaries who have the right to direct the investments of the account, or (2) once each calendar year for participants and beneficiaries who have accounts with the plan, but do not have control over the investment in the account.[39] Section 105 also provides that plan administrators of defined benefit plans must furnish benefit statements to participants and beneficiaries at least once every three years to any individual who has both a non-forfeitable accrued benefit and is employed by the employer maintaining the plan at the time the statement is furnished. Statements to participants in defined benefit plans must also be provided upon request. Pension benefit statements must indicate information such as amount of non-forfeitable benefits, accrued benefits, and the earliest date on which accrued benefits become non-forfeitable. Benefit statements covering a defined contribution plan must also include the value of each investment to which assets have been allocated in a participant or beneficiary's account.

5. Annual Funding Notice

Defined benefit plan administrators must also provide an annual plan funding notice.[40] While in previous years funding notices have been furnished by multiemployer plans, single-employer plans must provide this notice beginning in 2008. The required annual notices include information about the plan's funding policy, assets, and liabilities; a statement of the number of participants; and a general description of the benefits that are eligible to be guaranteed by the PBGC.[41] The notice must be provided to the PBGC, plan participants and beneficiaries, labor organizations representing such participants or beneficiaries, and, in the case of a multiemployer plan, to each employer who has an obligation to contribute to the plan.

6. Notice of Freedom to Divest Employer Securities

The PPA amended the disclosure provisions of ERISA to require plan administrators to provide participants with a notice of their eligibility to divest employer securities held in a defined contribution plan. Section 101(m) of ERISA requires plan administrators to provide this notice to applicable individuals at least 30 days before the date on which the individual is eligible to divest these securities.[42] The notice must inform the participant that he or she has the right to direct divestment of the employer securities and informed of the importance of diversifying the investment of retirement account assets. The notice must be written in a manner that can be understood by the average plan participant. It may be delivered in written, electronic, or other appropriate form that is reasonably accessible to the recipient.

C. Participation Requirements

ERISA restricts the amount of time an employee can be excluded from participating in a pension plan.[43] Under ERISA Section 202(a)(1)(A), an employee can only be excluded from an ERISA pension plan on account of age or service if the employee is under age 21 or has not yet completed a year of service.[44] The term "year of service" is defined as a 12-month period during which the employee has worked at least 1,000 hours.[45]

Alternatively, in the case of a plan under which a participant's benefits are 100% vested[46] after no more than two years of service, a plan may require two years of service prior to participating in the plan.[47] Plans maintained for employees of certain educational institutions which provide for 100% vesting after one year may condition participation on an employee's becoming 26 years old or completing one year of service, whichever is later.[48]

Once an employee becomes eligible to participate, a plan must enroll the employee no later than (1) the first day of the plan year or (2) six months after the date of satisfaction of the participation requirements, whichever is earlier.[49] ERISA also prohibits pension plans from excluding employees from participation in the plan after an employee has attained a certain age.[50]

D. Benefit Accrual

Section 204 of ERISA governs benefit accrual, which generally refers to the rate at which benefits are earned by a plan participant.[51] An "accrued benefit" is defined differently for defined benefit and defined contribution plans. For defined benefit plans, accrued benefit means an individual's benefit determined under the plan and expressed in the form of an annual benefit commencing at normal retirement age, subject to exceptions.[52] ERISA provides three primary methods for benefit accrual under a defined benefit plan:

Under the "133-1/3 rule," generally, a later rate of accrual for one year of plan participation cannot be more than 133-1/3 percent of the rate for any other plan year.

Under the "3% rule," a participant must accrue at least 3% of the participant's anticipated normal retirement benefit in each year of participation, up to a maximum of 3 3-1/3 years.

Under the "fractional rule," benefit accrual is focused on a worker's proportionate years of service under the plan. For example, if benefits can accrue for a maximum of 40 years up to the date of the plan's normal retirement age (such as 65), a worker starting under the plan at age 25 and working to age 60 would get 3 5/40 of the maximum credit toward a pension.[53]

These tests limit the amount of "backloading," a practice of providing a higher benefit accrual rate for later years of service than for earlier years. "Front loading" benefits (providing a higher accrual rate for earlier years of service than for later years) is permitted, but decreases in the rate of benefit accrual cannot be based on the participant's age.

In a defined contribution plan, the participant's accrued benefit is the balance in his or her account.[54] Participants begin accruing a benefit in a defined contribution plan once they have met the participation requirements under the terms of the plan.[55] However, if an employer makes contributions to an employee's account, the accrued benefit received may be treated differently for vesting purposes than the accrued benefit from employee contributions.[56]

1. Anti-cutback Rule

ERISA Section 204(g) prohibits plan amendments that eliminate or reduce benefits already accrued by plan participants.[57] This prohibition is commonly referred to as the "anti-cutback rule."[58] Benefits subject to the anti-cutback rule include basic accrued benefits, as well as any early retirement benefits, "retirement-type" subsidies, and other optional forms of benefits that an individual who has met certain requirements (as defined by the plan) is eligible to receive. However, the anti-cutback rule does not prevent a plan from freezing accrued benefits, reducing the rate at which benefits will accrue in the future, or eliminating future benefit accruals altogether.

Although an accrued benefit is generally defined in monetary terms, the Supreme Court has held that the anti-cutback rule applies not only to a particular sum of money, but to a plan amendment which hinders a participant's receipt of benefits.[59] In *Central Laborers' Pension Fund v. Heinz*,[60] a retired plan participant's benefits were suspended by the plan following a plan amendment that prohibited participants from engaging in the type of post-retirement employment he performed. The plaintiff claimed that this suspension violated ERISA's anti-cutback rule. The plan argued, among other things, that the anti-cutback rule applies only to amendments affecting the dollar amount the plan was obligated to pay, and that a mere suspension of benefits did not eliminate or reduce an accrued benefit. The Court rejected this argument and affirmed the decision of the lower court, stating that "as a matter of common sense, a participant's benefits cannot be understood without reference to the conditions imposed on receiving those benefits, and an amendment placing materially greater restrictions on the receipt of the benefit 'reduces' the benefit just as surely as a decrease in the size of the monthly benefit payment."[61]

2. *Benefit Accrual and Age Discrimination*

ERISA contains provisions designed to prevent age discrimination in benefit accrual.[62] Section 204(b)(1)(H) of ERISA prohibits a defined benefit plan from ceasing accruals or reducing the rate of accrual on account of the employee's age. Section 204(b)(2)(A) of ERISA provides that for defined contribution plans, allocations to an employee's account may not cease, and the rate at which amounts are allocated to an employee's account may not be reduced on account of age.

Over the past few years, several courts have evaluated these provisions in determining whether cash balance plans[63] are age-discriminatory. Discrimination has been alleged, among other things, because of the structure of a cash balance plan, under which employees receive both pay credits and interest credits. After the employee terminates employment, pay credits will generally cease, but an employee will typically continue to earn interest credits. Because a younger employee has more time before retirement age in which to earn interest than an older employee, an accrued benefit may be greater for a younger employee. This result, some have argued, violates the age discrimination provisions. While multiple appellate courts have found cash balance plans not to violate the age discrimination provisions, some district courts have held to the contrary.[64]

The PPA amended the benefit accrual requirements of ERISA, as well as other federal laws, by adding new standards under which a plan can be considered inherently non-age discriminatory.[65] Under the act, a plan is not considered age discriminatory if a participant's entire accrued benefit, as determined under the plan's formula, is at least equal to that of any similarly situated, younger individual. A "similarly situated" individual is defined as an individual who is identical to the participant in every respect, including length of service, compensation, position, and work history, except for age. The PPA provides that cash balance plans do not discriminate against older workers if, among other things, benefits are fully vested after three years of service and interest credits do not exceed a market rate of return. In general, the new provisions regarding cash balance plans are effective for periods beginning on or after June 29, 2005. However, cash balance plans in existence prior to this date may still be subject to legal challenge.[66]

E. Minimum Vesting Standards

While benefit accrual refers to the amount of benefits earned under ERISA, vesting occurs when a plan participant's accrued benefit is considered to be nonforfeitable.[67] Once benefits have vested, the participant may be able to receive the vested portion of his or her retirement benefits even if he or she leaves the job before retirement. Vesting requirements apply only to benefits derived from employer contributions to a plan. Participant contributions to a pension plan must be automatically nonforfeitable to the participant. [68]

ERISA imposes two general vesting requirements: one depending on age and one depending on length of service. First, under Section 203(a) of ERISA, all plans must provide that the employees' rights to their "normal retirement benefits"[69] are fully vested upon attainment of "normal retirement age."[70] While a plan may choose a "normal retirement age" for purposes of determining when a participant's benefits vest, ERISA provides that this age must be the earlier of: (1) the time a participant attains normal retirement age as specified under a plan or (2) the later of the time the participant attains age 65 or the fifth anniversary of the time the participant commenced participation in the plan.[71]

Second, ERISA's vesting provisions also require benefits to vest based on an employee's years of service to the employer. Under ERISA § 203(b), a qualified defined benefit plan must meet one of two vesting schedules.[72] The first schedule is met if a participant's benefits are fully vested after five years of service, commonly referred to as five-year "cliff" vesting. Alternatively, a participant's benefits may vest under the following graded vesting schedule:[73]

Years of service[74]	Vesting percentage
3	20%
4	40%
5	60%
6	80%
7	100%

Most defined contribution plans are subject to similar vesting requirements. Exceptions include the SIMPLE 401(k) and the Safe Harbor 401(k) plans, in which participants are immediately vested in employer contributions. For other defined contribution plans, employers have a choice between two vesting schedules for employer contributions.[75] Under cliff vesting, participants must be 100% vested in employer contributions after no more than three years of service. Under graduated or graded vesting, an employee must be at least 20% vested after two years, 40% after three years, 60% after four years, 80% after five years, and 100% vested after six years. Both employer matching contributions (*i.e.*, employer plan contributions made on behalf of an employee and on account of an employee's elective contributions)[76] as well as employer nonelective contributions (such as profit-sharing contributions) must vest under these rules.

Breaks in Service

ERISA protects plan participants from losing credit for earlier service in cases in which workers leave their jobs and then return to work within five years.[77] Once an employee becomes eligible to participate in a pension plan, all years of service with the employer during which the employer maintained the plan (including service before becoming a plan participant) must be taken into account for purposes of determining how much service will be counted toward meeting the plan's vesting requirement. In the case of a nonvested participant, years of service before any break in service must be taken into account upon reemployment. In a defined contribution plan, if a participant who is not 100% vested incurs a break in service of less than five years and subsequently returns to work, all service after returning to work must be added to the pre-break service in determining the vested portion of the pre-break benefit. A break in service occurs in any year in which the employee completes less than 500 hours of service. Generally, workers will not incur a break in service for up to one year's absence due to pregnancy, childbirth, infant care, or adoption.[78]

F. Benefit Protections for Spouses

The *Retirement Equity Act of 1984* (REA)[79] amended ERISA to increase pension protections for the survivors of deceased plan participants. As amended by the REA, ERISA requires defined benefit plans and money purchase plans to provide preretirement and postretirement survivor annuities to married employees unless a written election to waive the survivor annuity is signed by both the employee and his or her spouse.[80] In the event of divorce, ERISA requires plan administrators to honor qualified domestic relations orders (QDROs) issued by state courts that divide the pension or account balance between the two parties.[81] This requirement ensures that a court order awarding a share of a vested pension benefit to the former spouse of a divorced plan participant will be honored by the plan.

1. Preretirement Survivor Benefits

ERISA requires defined benefit plans to provide a survivor annuity to the spouse of a vested active participant or vested former participant. The cost of the preretirement survivor annuity may be paid by the employer or passed on to covered participants through reduced benefits or increased contributions. To waive the preretirement survivor benefit, both participant and spouse must sign a waiver form. The plan can defer payment of the survivor annuity until the month in which the deceased participant would have reached the plan's earliest retirement age. Profit-sharing plans (including 401(k) plans) and stock bonus plans must provide for automatic payment of the participant's vested account balance to his or her spouse upon the death of the participant unless both parties designate an alternate beneficiary in writing. If either a profit-sharing plan or stock bonus plan offers a life annuity option, it must provide a pre-retirement survivor annuity.

2. Postretirement Survivor Benefits

ERISA requires the default form of benefit paid to a married participant in a defined benefit plan to be a joint and survivor annuity that provides a life annuity to the survivor equal to at least 50% of the joint benefit paid while the participant was living. Beginning in 2008, the PPA requires plans to offer a 75% survivor annuity option if the plan's survivor annuity is less than 75%, and to offer a 50% survivor annuity option if the plan's survivor annuity is greater than 75%.[82] Waiving the survivor benefit requires the written consent of both the participant and spouse. The participant and spouse must have at least 90 days ending on the annuity starting date to waive the survivor annuity. The decision to waive the survivor annuity also can be revoked during this period.

Because a joint and survivor annuity is based on the joint life expectancy of the participant and spouse instead of a single life, the amount of the joint annuity is lower than it would be if it were a single-life annuity. Once a joint and survivor annuity is in effect and the retirement annuity has commenced, the spouse to whom the participant was married on the date that the annuity started is entitled to the survivor annuity, even if the couple is no longer married when the participant dies. Before the annuity begins, the employer must provide each participant with a written notice that states:

the terms and conditions of the qualified joint and survivor annuity;
the right of the participant and spouse to decline the survivor annuity and the effect of the decision;
the rights of the spouse; and
the right to reverse the decision and the effect of reversing it.

3. Qualified Domestic Relations Orders

The REA of 1984 amended ERISA to allow plans to honor state court orders awarding a share of a worker's pension to a former spouse.[83] ERISA sets forth procedures the plan administrator must follow to determine if a court order is a *qualified domestic relations order* (QDRO). Payments to the former spouse of a participant may begin when the participant becomes eligible to retire, even if the participant is still employed.

A QDRO must specify:

the name and last known address of the participant and each person to receive money,
the amount or percentage of the participant's benefits to be paid to each person,
the number of payments or the time period to which the order applies, and
each plan to which the order relates.

A QDRO generally will qualify only if it does *not* require the plan to:

provide a form of benefit not otherwise provided by the plan,
pay more benefits than it would have paid in the absence of the order, or
pay benefits that the plan must already pay to another beneficiary because of an earlier QDRO.

The PPA directed the Secretary of Labor to issue regulations to clarify whether a domestic relations order that supersedes or revises an earlier QDRO will be considered to be qualified, and to state the conditions under which a QDRO will not be treated as qualified because of the time at which it was issued.[84]

G. Buyouts, Mergers, and Consolidations

If a company is purchased by another firm, participants and beneficiaries in the acquired company may not be denied pension benefits already earned, and PBGC insurance protections continue to apply to those benefits. In the event of a plan merger, consolidation, or transfer of plan assets or liabilities, the participant's benefit must be equal to, or greater than, the benefit to which the participant would have been entitled had the plan been terminated immediately before the merger, consolidation, or transfer.[85]

H. Plan Funding

To ensure that sufficient money is available to pay promised pension benefits to participants and beneficiaries, ERISA sets rules that require plan sponsors to fully fund the pension liabilities of defined benefit plans.[86] These rules were substantially modified by the PPA. The funding requirements of ERISA recognize that pension liabilities are long-term liabilities. Consequently, plan liabilities need not be funded immediately, but instead can be amortized (paid off with interest) over a period of years. Single-employer plans generally are required to amortize initial past service liabilities and past service liabilities arising under plan amendments over no more than seven years. Defined contribution plans do not promise a specific benefit, and so these plans have no funding requirements.

ERISA requires employers that sponsor defined benefit plans to fund the pension benefits that plan participants earn each year. This is referred to as funding the *normal cost* of the plan. In addition, DB plan sponsors must amortize the cost of any pension benefits granted to employees for past service, but for which no monies were set aside. Furthermore, if a DB plan retroactively increases the level of benefits by plan amendment, these new liabilities must be amortized as well. The assets of the pension plan must be kept in a trust that is separate from the employer's general assets. Assets in the pension trust fund are protected from the claims of creditors in the event that the plan sponsor files for bankruptcy.

1. Funding Requirements for Single-employer Plans

ERISA requires companies that sponsor defined benefit pension plans to fully fund the benefits that plan participants earn each year. If a plan is underfunded, the plan sponsor must amortize this unfunded liability over a period of years. The PPA established new rules for determining whether a defined benefit plan is fully funded, the contribution needed to fund the benefits that plan participants will earn in the current year, and the contribution to the plan that is required if previously earned benefits are not fully funded. In general, the new rules are effective with plan years beginning in 2008, but many provisions of the PPA will be phased in over several years.

a. Minimum Funding Standards for Single-Employer Plans

Pension plan liabilities extend many years into the future. Determining whether a pension is adequately funded requires converting the future stream of pension payments into the amount that would be needed today to pay off those liabilities all at once. This amount — the "present value" of the plan's liabilities — is then compared with the value of the plan's assets. An underfunded plan is one in which the value of the plan's assets falls short of the present value of its liabilities. Converting a future stream of payments (or income) into a present value requires the future payments (or income) to be discounted using an appropriate interest rate. Other things being equal, the *higher* the interest rate, the *smaller* the present value of the future payments (or income), and vice versa.

When fully phased in, the new funding requirements established by the PPA will require plan assets to be equal to 100% of plan liabilities. Any unfunded liability will have to be amortized over no more than seven years. Sponsors of severely underfunded plans that are at risk of defaulting on their obligations will be required to fund their plans according to special rules that will result in higher employer contributions to the plan. Plan sponsors are allowed to use credit earned for past contributions (called "credit balances") to offset required contributions, but only if the plan is funded at 80% or more. The value of credit balances must be adjusted to reflect changes in the market value of plan assets since the date the contributions that created the credit balances were made.

A plan sponsor's minimum required contribution is based on the plan's *target normal cost* and the difference between the plan's *funding target* and the value of the plan's assets. The target normal cost is the present value of all benefits that plan participants will accrue during the year. The funding target is the present value of all benefits — including early retirement benefits — already accrued by plan participants as of the beginning of the plan year. If a plan's assets are less than the funding target, the plan has an *unfunded liability*. This liability — less any permissible credit balances — must be amortized in annual installments over no more than seven years. The plan sponsor's minimum required annual contribution is the plan's target normal cost for the plan year, but not less than zero. The 100% funding target is being phased in at 92% in 2008, 94% in 2009, 96% in 2010, and 100% in 2011 and later years. The phase-in does not apply to underfunded plans that were required to make deficit reduction contributions in 2007.[87] Those plans have a 100% funding target in 2008.

ERISA requires plans to discount future liabilities using three different interest rates, depending on the length of time until the liabilities must be paid.[88] A short- term interest rate is used to calculate the present value of liabilities that will come due within five years. A mid-term interest rate is used for liabilities that will come due in five to 20 years, and a long-term interest rate is applied to liabilities that will come due in more than 20 years. The Secretary of the Treasury determines these rates, which are derived from a "yield curve" of investment-grade corporate bonds averaged over the most recent 24 months.[89] The yield curve is being phased in over three years beginning in 2007. It will replace the four-year average of corporate bond rates established under the *Pension Funding Equity Act of 2004*,[90] which expired on December 31, 2005.[91]

b. "At risk" Plans

Pension plans that are determined to be at risk of defaulting on their liabilities must use specific actuarial assumptions to determine plan liabilities.[92] A plan is deemed to be at-risk if it is unable to pass either of two tests. Under the first test, a plan is at-risk if it is less than 70% funded under the "worst-case scenario" assumptions that (1) the employer is not permitted to use credit balances to reduce its cash contribution and (2) employees will retire at the earliest possible date and will choose to take the most expensive form of benefit. If a plan does not pass this test, it will be deemed to be at-risk *unless* it is at least 80% funded under standard actuarial assumptions. This latter test will be phased in over four years, with the minimum funding requirement starting at 65% in 2008 and rising to 70% in 2009, 75% in 2010, and 80% in 2011. If a plan passes either of these two tests, it is not deemed to be at-risk; however, it is required to make up its funding shortfall over no more than seven years. Plans that have been at-risk for at least two of the previous four years also will be subject to an additional "loading factor" equal to 4% of the plan's liabilities plus $700 per participant, which is added to the plan sponsor's required contribution to the plan. Plan years prior to 2008 will not count for this determination. Plans with 500 or fewer participants in the preceding year are exempt from the at-risk funding requirements.

c. Mortality Tables

To estimate a pension plan's future obligations, the plan's actuaries use mortality tables to project the number of participants who will claim a pension and the average length of time that participants and their surviving beneficiaries will receive pension payments. ERISA requires the Secretary of the Treasury to prescribe the mortality tables to be used for these estimates.[93] Large plans can petition the IRS to use a plan-specific mortality table.

2. Valuation of Plan Assets

Prior to enactment of the PPA, a plan sponsor could determine the value of a plan's assets using actuarial valuations, which can differ from the current market value of those assets. For example, in an actuarial valuation, the plan's investment returns could be "smoothed" (averaged) over a five-year period, and the average asset value could range from 80% to 120% of the fair market value. Averaging asset values reduces volatility in the measurement of plan assets that can be caused by year-to-year fluctuations in interest rates and the rate of return on investments. Averaging therefore reduces the year-to-year volatility in the plan sponsor's required minimum contributions to the pension plan. The PPA narrowed the range for actuarial valuations to no less than 90% and no more than 110% of fair market value and it reduced the maximum smoothing period to two years. Plans with more than 100 participants are required to use the first day of the plan year as the basis for calculations of plan assets and liabilities. Plans with 100 or fewer participants can choose another date.

Plan Contributions and Credit Balances

Within limits, plan sponsors can offset required current contributions with previous contributions. However, these so-called "credit balances" can be used to reduce the plan sponsor's minimum required contribution to the plan only if the plan's assets are at least 80% of the funding target, not counting prefunding balances that have arisen since the PPA became effective.[94] Existing credit balances and new prefunding balances must both be subtracted from assets in determining the "adjusted funding target attainment" percentage that is used to determine whether certain benefits can be paid and whether benefit increases are allowed. Credit balances also have to be adjusted for investment gains and losses since the date of the original contribution that created the credit balance. Credit balances must be separated into balances carried over from 2007 and balances resulting from contributions in 2008 and later years.

3. Benefit Limitations in Underfunded Plans

ERISA places limits on (1) plan amendments that would increase benefits, (2) benefit accruals, and (3) benefit distribution options (such as lump sums) in single-employer defined benefit plans that fail to meet specific funding thresholds.[95]

a. Shutdown Benefits

Shutdown benefits are payments made to employees when a plant or factory is shut down. These benefits typically are negotiated between employers and labor unions, and usually they are not prefunded. ERISA prohibits shut-down benefits and other "contingent event benefits" from being paid by pension plans that are funded at less than 60% of full funding unless the employer makes a prescribed additional contribution to the plan. The PBGC guarantee for such benefits is phased in over a five-year period commencing when the event occurs.[96]

b. Restrictions on Benefit Accruals

ERISA requires benefit accruals to cease in plans funded at less than 60% of full funding. Once a plan is funded above 60%, the employer — and the union in a collectively bargained plan — must decide how to credit past service accruals. This provision does not apply if the employer makes an additional contribution prescribed by statute.

c. Restrictions on Benefit Increases

Plan amendments that increase benefits are prohibited if the plan is funded at less than 80% of the full funding level, unless the employer makes additional contributions to fully fund the new benefits. Benefit increases include — but are not limited to — increases in the rate of benefit accrual and increasing the rate at which benefits become vested.

d. Restrictions on Lump Sum Distributions

Lump-sum distributions are prohibited if the plan is funded at less than 60% of the full funding level or if the plan sponsor is in bankruptcy and the plan is less than 100% funded. If the plan is funded at more than 60% but less than 80%, the plan may distribute as a lump sum no more than half of the participant's accrued benefit.

e. Notice to Participants

ERISA requires plan sponsors to notify participants of restrictions on shutdown benefits, lump-sum distributions, or suspension of benefit accruals within 30 days of the plan being subject to any of these restrictions. The restrictions on benefits in underfunded plans are effective in 2008, but not before 2010, for collectively bargained plans.

4. Lump-sum Distributions

ERISA requires defined benefit pensions to offer participants the option to receive their accrued benefit as a life annuity: a series of monthly payments guaranteed for life. Many defined benefit plans also offer participants the option to take their accrued benefit as a lump sum at the time they separate from the employer. The amount of a lump-sum distribution from a defined benefit pension is inversely related to the interest rate used to calculate the present value of the benefit that has been accrued under the plan: the higher the interest rate, the smaller the lump sum and vice versa. To protect employees' accrued benefits, ERISA prescribes interest rates and mortality tables to be used in determining the minimum value of a participant's benefit expressed as a lump sum. Before the PPA, minimum lump-sum values were calculated using the interest rate on 30-year Treasury bonds. As amended by the PPA, ERISA requires lump-sum payments from defined benefit plans to be no less than the amount that would result from using the applicable corporate bond interest rate.[97] It requires plans that use an interest rate that results in larger lump sums to treat these larger payments as a subsidy to plan participants, which must be funded by the plan sponsor. The new rules for lump sums are being phased in over five years, beginning in 2008.

When fully phased in, minimum permissible lump-sum distributions will be based on a three-segment interest rate yield curve, derived from the rates of return on investment-grade corporate bonds of varying maturities. Plan participants of different ages will have their lump-sum distributions calculated using different interest rates. Other things being equal, a lump-sum distribution paid to a worker who is near the plan's normal retirement age will be calculated using a lower interest rate than will be used for a younger worker. As a result, all else being equal, an older worker will receive a larger lump sum than a similarly situated younger worker. The interest rates used to calculate lump sums will be based on *current* bond rates rather than the three-year *weighted average* rate used to calculate the plan's funding target. Plans funded at less than 60% are prohibited from paying lump-sum distributions. Plans funded at 60% to 80% can pay no more than half of a participant's accrued benefit as a lump-sum distribution.

The PPA also established a new interest rate floor for testing whether a lump sum paid from a defined benefit plan complies with the benefit limitations under IRC §41 5(b).[98] In general, IRC §415(b) limits the annual single-life annuity payable from a qualified defined benefit plan to the lesser of 100% of average compensation over three years or $185,000 (in 2008). A benefit paid as a lump sum must be converted to an equivalent annuity value for purposes of applying this limit. As amended by the PPA, ERISA requires plans making this calculation to use an interest rate that is no lower than the highest of (1) 5.5%, (2) the rate that results in a benefit of no more than 105% of the benefit that would be provided if the interest rate required for determining a lump sum distribution were used, or (3) the interest rate specified in the plan documents.[99]

5. Funding Requirements for Multiemployer Plans

A multiemployer plan is a collectively bargained plan maintained by several employers — usually within the same industry — and a labor union. Multiemployer defined benefit plans are subject to funding requirements that differ from those for single-employer plans. The PPA established a new set of rules for improving the funding of multiemployer plans that the law defines as being in "endangered" or "critical" status.[100] These new requirements will remain in effect through 2014.

As amended by the PPA, ERISA requires each multiemployer plan to certify the plan's current funding status and project its funding status for the following six years within 90 days after the start of the plan year. If the plan is underfunded, it has 30 days after the certification date to notify participants and eight months to develop a funding schedule that meets the statutory funding requirements and to present it to the parties of the plan's collective bargaining agreement. Multiemployer plans must amortize any increases in plan liabilities that are due to benefit increases or to changes in the actuarial assumptions used by the plan over a period of 15 years.

The PPA increased the limit on tax-deductible employer contributions to multiemployer plans to 140% of the plan's current liability (up from 100%), and it eliminated the 25%-of-compensation combined limit on contributions to defined benefit and defined contribution plans. The PPA also allows the Internal Revenue Service to permit multiemployer plans that project a funding deficiency within ten years to extend the amortization schedule for paying off its liabilities by five years, with a further five-year extension permissible. It requires the plans to adopt a recovery plan and to use specific interest rates for plan funding calculations.

a. Requirements for Underfunded Multiemployer Plans

The PPA established mandatory procedures, effective through 2014, to improve the funding of seriously underfunded multiemployer plans. A multiemployer plan is considered to be *endangered* if it is less than 80% funded **or** if the plan is projected to have a funding deficiency within seven years. A plan that is less than 80% funded **and** is projected to have a funding deficiency within seven years is considered to be *seriously endangered.* An endangered plan has one year to implement a "funding improvement plan" designed to reduce the amount of under-funding. Endangered plans have 10 years to improve their funding. They must improve their funding percentage by one-third of the difference between 100% funding and the plan's funded percentage from the earlier of (1) two years after the adoption of the funding improvement plan or (2) the first plan year after the expiration of collective bargaining agreements that cover at least 75% of the plan's active participants.

Seriously endangered plans that are less than 70% funded have 15 years to improve their funding. They must improve their funding percentage by one-fifth of the difference between 100% funding and the plan's funded percentage from the earlier of (1) two years after the adoption of the funding improvement plan or (2) the first plan year after the expiration of collective bargaining agreements that cover at least 75% of the plan's active participants. A plan that is endangered or seriously endangered may not increase benefits. If the parties to the collective bargaining agreement are not able to agree on a funding improvement plan, a default funding schedule applies that will reduce future benefit accruals. A multiemployer plan is not endangered in any plan year in which the required funding percentages are met.

A multiemployer plan is considered to be in *critical status* if (1) it is less than 65% funded and it has a projected funding deficiency within five years or will be unable to pay benefits within seven years; (2) it has a projected funding deficiency within four years or will be unable to pay benefits within five years (regardless of its funded percentage); or (3) its liabilities for inactive participants are greater than its liabilities for active participants, its contributions are less than carrying costs, and a funding deficiency is projected within five years. A plan in critical status has one year to develop a rehabilitation plan designed to reduce the amount of underfunding.

b. Reductions in Adjustable Benefits

In general, ERISA's anti-cutback rule prohibits reductions in accrued, vested benefits. The PPA relaxed the anti-cutback rule so that multiemployer plans in critical status are permitted to reduce or eliminate early retirement subsidies and other "adjustable benefits" to help improve their funding status if this is agreed to by the bargaining parties. Benefits payable at normal retirement age cannot be reduced, and plans are not permitted to cut any benefits of participants who retired before they were notified that the plan is in critical status. Adjustable benefits include certain optional forms of benefit payment, disability benefits, early retirement benefits, joint and survivor annuities (if the survivor benefit exceeds 50%), and benefit increases adopted or effective less than five years before the plan entered critical status.

c. Disclosure Requirements

As amended by the PPA, ERISA requires multiemployer plans to send funding notices to participants within 120 days after the end of the plan year. The Department of Labor will post information from plans' annual reports on its website, and plans are required to provide certain information to participants on request. For plans in endangered or critical status, the plan actuary must certify that the funding improvement is on schedule. Annual reports must contain information on funding improvement plans or rehabilitation plans. Notification must be provided to participants, beneficiaries, bargaining parties, the PBGC, and the Secretary of Labor within 30 days after the plan determines that it is in endangered or critical status.

I. Fiduciary Responsibility

ERISA imposes certain obligations on plan fiduciaries, persons who are generally responsible for the management and operation of employee benefit plans. ERISA Section 3(21)(A) provides that a person is a "fiduciary" to the extent that the person: (1) exercises any discretionary authority or control with respect to the management of the plan or exercises any authority with respect to the management or disposition of plan assets; (2) renders investment advice for a fee or other compensation with respect to any plan asset or has any authority or responsibility to do so;[101] or (3) has any discretionary responsibility in the administration of the plan.[102] Every plan governed by ERISA must have one or more named fiduciaries, and these fiduciaries must be named in the plan document.[103] Section 404(a)(1) of ERISA establishes the duties owed by a fiduciary to participants and beneficiaries of a plan. This section identifies four standards of conduct: (1) a duty of loyalty, (2) a duty of prudence, (3) a duty to diversify investments, and (4) a duty to follow plan documents to the extent that they comply with ERISA.[104]

1. Duty of Loyalty

Section 404(a)(1)(A) of ERISA requires plan fiduciaries to discharge their duties "solely in the interest of the participants and beneficiaries" and for the "exclusive purpose" of providing benefits to participants and beneficiaries and defraying reasonable expenses of administering the plan.[105] The duty of loyalty applies in situations where the fiduciary is confronted with a potential conflict of interest, for instance, when a pension plan trustee has responsibilities to both the plan and the entity (such as the employer or union) sponsoring the plan.[106]

However, just because an ERISA fiduciary engages in a transaction that incidentally benefits the fiduciary or a third party does not necessarily mean that a fiduciary breach has occurred.[107] One case to address this idea is *Donovan v. Bierwirth*, a case under which pension plan trustees, who were also corporate officers, were responsible for deciding whether they should tender shares of company stock in order to thwart a hostile takeover attempt.[108] The trustees not only decided against tendering the stock, but also decided to purchase additional company stock for the pension plan. In finding that the trustees had breached their fiduciary duties, the court in *Donovan* noted that it is not a breach of fiduciary duty if a trustee who, after careful and impartial investigation, makes a decision that while benefitting the plan, also incidentally benefits the corporation, or the fiduciaries themselves. However, fiduciary decisions must be made with an "eye single to the interests of the participants and beneficiaries."[109] The court articulated that the trustees have a duty to "avoid placing themselves in a position where their acts as officers and directors of the corporation will prevent their functioning with the complete loyalty to participants demanded of them as trustees of a pension plan."[110]

A plan fiduciary must also act with the "exclusive purpose" of "defraying reasonable expenses of administering the plan."[111] The Department of Labor has stated that "in choosing among potential service providers, as well as in monitoring and deciding whether to retain a service provider, the trustees must objectively assess the qualifications of the service provider, the quality of the work product, and the reasonableness of the fees charged in light of the services provided."[112]

On November 16, 2007, the Department of Labor issued a final regulation that revises the Form 5500, which plans file each year to report their funding status and other financial information that ERISA requires to be disclosed to the Department. The regulation will require disclosure of information regarding the fees paid by the plan to administrators, record keepers, and other service providers.[113] On December 13, 2007, the Department of Labor published a proposed regulation that would require service providers to disclose to plan fiduciaries, in advance of entering into a contract with the plan, all fees and any other direct or indirect compensation that the service provider would receive while under contract to the plan.[114]

2. Duty of Prudence

Section 404(a)(1)(B) of ERISA requires fiduciaries to act "with the care, skill, prudence, and diligence under the circumstances then prevailing that a prudent man would use in the conduct of an enterprise of a like character with like aims."[115] When examining whether a fiduciary has violated the duty of prudence, courts typically examine the process that a fiduciary undertook in reaching a decision involving plan assets.[116] If a fiduciary has taken the appropriate procedural steps, the success or failure of an investment can be irrelevant to a duty of prudence inquiry.[117]

Regulations promulgated by the Department of Labor provide clarification as to the duty of prudence in regard to investment decisions. These regulations indicate that a fiduciary can satisfy his duty of prudence under ERISA by giving "appropriate consideration" to the facts and circumstances that the fiduciary knows or should know are relevant to an investment or investment course of action.[118] "Appropriate consideration" includes (1) "a determination by the fiduciary that the particular investment or investment course of action is reasonably designed, as part of the portfolio ... to further the purposes of the plan, taking into consideration the risk of loss and the opportunity for gain (or other return) associated with the investment," and (2) consideration of the portfolio's composition with regard to diversification, the liquidity and current return of the portfolio relative to the anticipated cash flow requirements of the plan, and the projected return of the portfolio relative to the plan's funding objectives.[119]

3. Duty to Diversify Investments

Section 404(a)(1)(C) of ERISA requires fiduciaries to diversify the investments of a plan "so as to minimize the risk of large losses, unless under the circumstances it is clearly prudent not to do so."[120] In general, it is believed that fiduciaries should not invest an unreasonably large proportion of a plan's portfolio in a single security, in a single type of security, or in various securities dependent upon the success of a single enterprise or upon conditions in a single locality.[121]

Courts have agreed that ERISA Section 404(a)(1)(C) does not create a diversification obligation in terms of fixed criteria, but instead requires a determination based on the specific facts of each individual case.[122] In *GIW Industries, Inc. v. Trevor Stewart,*[123] the court concluded that the defendant investment manager breached its duty to diversify investments by investing too heavily in long-term government bonds. By investing 70 percent of the plan's assets in long-term bonds rather than short-term bonds, the firm exposed the fund to a greater degree of risk. Expert testimony had indicated that short-term bonds or bonds with staggered maturity dates would have minimized exposure if the bonds were sold before maturity. The court maintained that Trevor Stewart's investment exposed the fund "to greater risk of cash outflows than was prudent."[124]

Similarly, in *Brock v. Citizens Bank of Clovis,*[125] the Tenth Circuit determined that trustees of the Citizens Bank of Clovis Pension Plan breached their duty to diversify investments by investing over 65 percent of the plan's assets in commercial real estate mortgages. The court maintained that the trustees' significant investment in one type of security exposed the plan to a multitude of risks. Moreover, the court found that the trustees failed to establish that the investments were prudent notwithstanding the lack of diversification. However, in *Metzler v. Graham,*[126] the court found that a plan trustee had not breached his duty under Section 404(a)(1)(C), even though he had invested more than half of the plan's assets in one piece of real estate. While the court found that the trustee had not diversified investments, the court concluded that the lack of diversification of the plan's investments was prudent under the facts and circumstances of the case.[127]

4. Duty to Act in Accordance with Plan Documents

Section 404(a)(1)(D) of ERISA requires fiduciaries to discharge their duties "in accordance with the documents and instruments governing the plan insofar as such documents and instruments are consistent with [ERISA]."[128] Courts have interpreted this section to apply not only to a document or instrument that establishes a plan or maintains a plan, but also to other writings that have a substantive effect on the plan.[129] These writings have included investment management agreements, collective bargaining agreements, and even internal memoranda regarding the sale of plan assets.[130]

Under Section 404(a)(1)(d), if a plan provision conflicts with ERISA, a fiduciary is obligated to ignore the plan provision.[131] Courts have evaluated this requirement in the context of when compliance with a plan provision leads to a breach of other fiduciary duties. The Department of Labor has argued that "if obeying a plan provision requires the fiduciary to act imprudently and disloyally in violation of ERISA section 404(a)(1)(A) and (B) ... the provision is not consistent with ERISA and the fiduciary has a duty to disregard it."[132] This situation was addressed in *Tittle v. Enron*,[133] in which the pension plan in question required employer contributions to be made "primarily in Enron stock." The court in *Enron* held that the plan fiduciaries had a duty to ignore this provision if it would be imprudent to follow it.[134]

In interpreting Section 404(a)(1)(D), courts have also held that fiduciaries do not breach the duty to act in accordance with plan documents if their failure to follow such documents results from erroneous interpretations made in good faith. In *Morgan v. Independent Drivers Association Pension Plan*,[135] the Tenth Circuit found that the trustees of a pension plan did not violate Section 404(a)(1)(D) because their decision to terminate the plan based on an erroneous interpretation of the effect of a new plan funding method was both considered in good faith and based on consultation with experts.

5. Prohibited Transactions

In addition to requiring plan fiduciaries to adhere to certain standards of conduct, ERISA prohibits fiduciaries from engaging in specified transactions deemed likely to injure a pension plan.[136] Engaging in a prohibited transaction is a per se violation of ERISA. Thus, in evaluating a fiduciary's role in a prohibited transaction, it may be considered irrelevant to examine whether the transaction would be considered prudent had it occurred between independent parties.[137]

Section 406(a) of ERISA bars certain transactions between a plan and a party in interest[138] with respect to a plan. Subject to certain exemptions,[139] a fiduciary must not cause a plan to engage in any transaction with a party in interest if the fiduciary knows or should know that the transaction is a:

sale or exchange, or leasing, of any property;
lending of money or other extension of credit;
furnishing of goods, services, or facilities;
transfer or use of any plan assets; or

acquisition, on behalf of the plan, of any employer security or employer real property in violation of ERISA § 407, which limits the amount of employer securities and property that may be held by a plan.

Section 406(b) prohibits certain transactions between a plan and a plan fiduciary. A fiduciary may not:

deal with the assets of the plan in his own interest or for his own account;

act in any transaction involving the plan on behalf of a party (or represent a party) whose interests are adverse to the interests of the plan or the interests of its participants or beneficiaries, or

receive any consideration for his own personal account from any party dealing with such plan in connection with a transaction involving the assets of the plan.[140]

ERISA also places a limit on the amount of investment in the sponsoring employer's stock and property held in a defined benefit plan. Section 407 generally provides that a plan may not invest in securities of an employer unless they are "qualifying employer securities."[141] Further, under this section, a plan may not acquire or hold employer real property unless it is "qualifying employer real property."[142] However, a plan may not acquire qualifying employer securities or qualifying employer property, if immediately after the acquisition, the aggregate fair market value of employer securities and employer real property held by the plan is more than 10% of the fair market value of the assets of the plan.

The Section 407 requirements generally do not apply to defined contribution plans, unless the plan requires a portion of an elective deferral to be invested in qualifying employer securities or qualifying employer real property.[143] However, the PPA created new diversification requirements for qualifying employer securities held in defined contribution plans. Section 204(j) of ERISA provides that an individual must be allowed to elect to direct a plan to divest employee contributions and elective deferrals invested in employer securities, and reinvest these amounts in other investment options.[144] A plan must offer at least three investment options (besides employer securities) to which an individual may direct the proceeds from the divestment. Individuals must be allowed to diversify their employee contributions out of employer stock as often as other investment changes are allowed, but at least quarterly. In addition, employees who have completed three years of service must also be allowed to diversify employer matching contributions and employer nonelective contributions out of employer stock. This requirement is phased in over three years for existing amounts contributed in plan years before 2007.[145] The section also provides that except as provided in regulations, plans cannot impose restrictions on employer stock investment or diversification that are not imposed on other plan investments.

ERISA provides for various exemptions from the prohibited transactions provisions. Section 408(a) directs the Secretary of Labor to establish a procedure for granting administrative exemptions for certain individuals and classes.[146] The section provides that the Secretary may not grant an exemption under this section unless it is (1) administratively feasible, (2) in the interests of the plan and of its participants and beneficiaries, and (3) protective of the rights of participants and beneficiaries of the plan. The Labor Department has promulgated regulations outlining the procedures for filing and processing prohibited transaction exemption applications.[147]

Section 408(b) of ERISA provides a number of statutory exemptions. These exemptions, found in Section 408(b), include certain loans to participants and beneficiaries (so long as certain conditions are met);[148] reasonable arrangements with parties in interest for office space or legal, accounting, or other services needed for the establishment or operation of the plan; certain plan investments (in the form of deposits) made in banks or in similar financial institutions whose employees are covered by the plans; as well as the purchase of life insurance, health insurance, or annuities from a qualifying insurer who is the employer maintaining the plan.

6. Investment Advice

Prior to the PPA, ERISA's prohibited transaction restrictions were believed to have discouraged the provision of investment advice.[149] Because it was perceived that "[v]irtually any transaction could fall within one of these [prohibited transaction] categories," individuals were reluctant to provide investment advice to plan participants.[150] The PPA amended both ERISA and the Internal Revenue Code to add a statutory prohibited transaction exemption with regard to providing investment advice. This exemption allows fiduciaries to provide investment advice without fear of fiduciary liability under the prohibited transaction provisions.

Section 408(g)(1) of ERISA, as added by Section 601(a)(2) of the PPA, states that the act's prohibited transaction restrictions shall not apply to transactions involving investment advice if such advice is provided by a fiduciary adviser pursuant to an "eligible investment advice arrangement." An "eligible investment advice arrangement" is defined as an arrangement that either

(1) provides that any fees (including any commission or other compensation) received by the fiduciary adviser for investment advice or with respect to the sale, holding, or acquisition of any security or other property for purposes of investment of plan assets do not vary depending on the basis of any investment option selected, or
(2) uses a computer model under an investment advice program meeting the requirements of Section 408(g)(3) in connection with the provision of investment advice by a fiduciary adviser to a participant or beneficiary.

To be considered an "eligible investment advice arrangement," an arrangement must meet other requirements identified in subsequent paragraphs of Section 408(g). These requirements include the following: the express authorization of the arrangement by a plan fiduciary other than the person offering the investment advice program, any person providing investment options under the plan, or any affiliate of either; the performance of an annual audit of the arrangement by an independent auditor; compliance with various disclosure requirements; the writing of participant notifications in a clear and conspicuous manner; and the maintenance of any records showing compliance with the relevant provisions of Section 408(g) for not less than six years. If investment advice is provided through the use of a computer model, such model must also meet certain specified requirements.[151]

7. Fiduciary Duty and Participant-Controlled Investment

Under Section 404(c) of ERISA, if a defined contribution plan permits a participant or beneficiary "to exercise control over the assets in his account," a fiduciary will not be liable for any loss which may result from the participant's or beneficiary's investment choices. However, in order for a fiduciary to be immune from liability, a plan must meet certain requirements.[152] Labor Department regulations describe two basic requirements for a plan to be considered a "404(c) plan."[153] First, a plan must provide the participant or beneficiary the opportunity to exercise control over the assets in the individual's account.[154] Individuals must, among other things, have a "reasonable opportunity to give investment instructions" as well as "the opportunity to obtain sufficient information to make informed decisions" about investment alternatives under the plan.[155]

Second, a plan must allow a participant or beneficiary to choose from a "broad range of investment alternatives."[156] A participant or beneficiary is deemed to have access to this range of alternatives if, among other things, the individual has the opportunity to "materially affect" the potential return and the degree of risk on the portion of the individual account with respect to which he is permitted to exercise control.[157] In addition, a participant or beneficiary must be given a choice of at least three investment alternatives, each of which is diversified, has different risk and return characteristics, and which, in the aggregate, enable the participant to achieve a portfolio with risk and return characteristics that are "normally appropriate" for the participant or beneficiary.[158]

In addition, in order for a fiduciary to be immune from liability under Section 404(c), a participant or beneficiary must not only have the ability to exercise control of plan assets, but must also have taken the opportunity to "exercise independent control" with respect to the investment of assets in the individual's account. The 404(c) regulations provide guidance as to when a participant or beneficiary will be deemed to have exercised control over plan assets,[159] as well as certain circumstances under which a participant or beneficiary's exercise of control will not be considered "independent."[160]

8. Fiduciary Liability under ERISA Section 409

Plan fiduciaries may be personally liable if the fiduciary breaches a responsibility, duty, or obligation under ERISA.[161] Section 409 of ERISA provides that a fiduciary may be liable to a plan for any losses resulting from such breach and may be responsible for forfeiting to the plan any profits that have been made through the improper use of plan assets.[162] Besides this monetary relief available, a court may also award "equitable and remedial relief" as it deems appropriate.

In addition, Section 409(b) provides that a fiduciary is not liable with respect to a breach of fiduciary duty "if such breach was committed before he became or after he ceased to be a fiduciary." Courts have found that fiduciaries are not liable for losses caused by an imprudent investment made prior to when the individual assumed fiduciary responsibility.[163] Still, a fiduciary may have an obligation to rectify breaches of fiduciary duty committed by a previous fiduciary and may be liable if he or she fails to take remedial action.[164]

J. Administration and Enforcement

One of the primary goals in enacting ERISA was to "protect ... the interests of participants and ... beneficiaries" of employee benefit plans, and assure that participants receive promised benefits from their employers.[165] To this end, ERISA "provid[es] for appropriate remedies, sanctions, and ready access to the Federal courts."[166] ERISA contains an "integrated enforcement mechanism"[167] that is also "essential to accomplish Congress' purpose of creating a comprehensive statute for the regulation of employee benefit plans."[168] An integral part of the civil enforcement scheme is ERISA Section 502, which allows both private parties as well as government entities to bring various civil actions to enforce provisions of ERISA.[169]

1. Civil Enforcement under Section 502(a)

Section 502(a) authorizes civil actions under ERISA as well as the remedies available to a successful plaintiff. Civil actions under Section 502(a) include the following actions that may be brought by a participant or a beneficiary, or, in some cases, a plan fiduciary or the Secretary of Labor, to:

- redress the failure of a plan administrator to provide information required by ERISA's reporting and disclosure requirements or COBRA requirements (Section 502(a)(1)(A));
- recover benefits due to a participant or beneficiary under the terms of his plan, to enforce his rights or to clarify his rights to future benefits under the terms of the plan (Section 502(a)(1)(B));
- receive appropriate relief due to breaches of fiduciary duty (Section 502(a)(2));
- enjoin any act or practice which violates ERISA or the terms of the plan, as well as to obtain other appropriate equitable relief to redress such violations (Section 502(a)(3));
- collect civil penalties (Section 502(a)(6)).[170]

The Supreme Court has found the enforcement scheme under Section 502(a) to contain "exclusive" federal remedies. Accordingly, Section 502(a) may preempt state law under the jurisdictional doctrine of "complete preemption." As the Supreme Court has reasoned, Congress may so completely preempt a particular area that "any civil complaint raising [a] select group of claims is necessarily federal in character."[171] In other words, complete preemption can occur "when Congress intends that a federal statute preempt a field of law so completely that state law claims are considered to be converted into federal causes of action."[172] Under the doctrine of complete preemption, a state claim that conflicts with a federal statutory scheme may be removed to federal court.[173] In the context of ERISA, if a state law claim is considered within the scope of ERISA's 502(a) civil enforcement provisions, the state law claim is completely preempted. Under these circumstances, a plaintiff is limited to bringing a claim under Section 502 of ERISA and may only receive the remedies available under the federal statute.[174]

Courts have frequently examined the scope of the remedies available under Section 502(a), in light of preemption and other factors. Questions have arisen as to which plaintiffs are eligible to bring a Section 502(a) claim and what remedies are available to them. The following discussion addresses how the Supreme Court has evaluated various claims under Section 502.

2. Claims to Enforce Benefit Rights

Section 502(a)(1)(B) of ERISA authorizes a plaintiff (*i.e.*, a participant or a beneficiary in an ERISA plan) to bring an action against the plan to recover benefits under the terms of the plan, or to enforce or clarify the plaintiff's rights under the terms of the plan. Under this section, if a plaintiff's claim for benefits is improperly denied, the plaintiff may sue to recover the unpaid benefit. A plaintiff may also seek a declaration to preserve a right to future benefits or an injunction to prevent a future denial of benefits.[175]

In terms of monetary remedies, Section 502(a)(1)(B) provides that a successful plaintiff may receive the benefits the plaintiff would have been entitled to under the terms of the plan. Compensatory or punitive damages are not available. In addition, as Section 502 of ERISA is considered to contain "exclusive" federal remedies, Section 502(a)(1)(B) has been held to preempt state or common law causes of action that may provide for more generous remedies than what is available under ERISA. The preemption of these state law claims has been controversial, as it can significantly impact plaintiffs relative to their opportunity to recover various types of damages under state law. The question of which state law claims are preempted by ERISA 502(a)(1)(B) has been controversial and has received significant attention from the courts.

The Supreme Court in *Pilot Life v. Dedeaux*[176] evaluated whether a state law claim for wrongful denial of benefits was preempted by Sections 514 and 502 of ERISA.[177] The plaintiffs in *Pilot Life* claimed that the denial of disability benefits by insurers of ERISA-regulated plans violated a Mississippi common law relating to bad faith. In finding the state law claim preempted by

Section 502, the Court reasoned that the civil enforcement provisions of 502(a) of ERISA are intended to be the "exclusive vehicle" for actions asserting improper processing of a claim for benefits. Further, in explaining why state law claims (and remedies) were not available, the Court explained:

> ... the provisions of 502(a) set forth a comprehensive civil enforcement scheme that represents a careful balancing of the need for prompt and fair claims settlement procedures against the public interest in encouraging the formation of employee benefit plans ... the policy choices reflected in the inclusion of certain remedies and the exclusion of others under the federal scheme would be undermined if ERISA-plan participants and beneficiaries were free to obtain remedies under state law that Congress rejected in ERISA.[178]

In *Aetna Health Inc. v. Davila,*[179] two individuals sued their insurance carriers, claiming the carriers violated the Texas Health Care Liability Act when they failed to exercise ordinary care in denying benefit coverage.[180] The insurance carriers removed the cases to the federal district court and argued that Section 502(a)(1)(B) of ERISA completely preempted the respondents' causes of action.

At issue for the Supreme Court was whether the individual's causes of action were preempted by Section 502(a) of ERISA and, thus, removal to federal court was proper. Respondents argued, among other things, that their state law claim for violating the "duty of ordinary care" arises independently of any duty imposed under ERISA. However, the Court disagreed, finding that "respondents bring suit only to rectify a wrongful denial of benefits promised under ERISA-regulated plans and do not attempt to remedy any violation of a legal duty independent of ERISA." The Court, relying on its decision in *Pilot Life*, among other cases, explained that a state cause of action that "attempts to authorize" a larger remedy than ERISA Section 502(a) does not place it outside of an ERISA claim.[181]

3. Claims to Redress Breaches of Fiduciary Duty

Section 502(a)(2) of ERISA authorizes the Secretary of Labor, a participant, a beneficiary, or a plan fiduciary to bring a civil action caused by a breach of fiduciary duty under Section 409 of ERISA. That section makes a plan fiduciary personally liable for breaches against an ERISA plan, and a breaching fiduciary must make good to the plan "any losses to the plan resulting from a breach" and restore to the plan any profits made from using the assets of the plan in improper ways.[182] It also subjects such a fiduciary to other relief as a court may deem appropriate, including removal of the fiduciary.

One controversial issue with respect to breach of fiduciary duty claims under ERISA has been that while an individual plaintiff (*e.g.*, a plan participant) may bring a civil action under Section 502 (a) (2), the Supreme Court has found that any recovery must "inure ... to the benefit of a plan as a whole."[183] In *Massachusetts Mutual Life Insurance Co. v. Russell*,[184] the Supreme Court evaluated whether a plan beneficiary could bring a civil action for monetary damages against a plan fiduciary who had been responsible for the improper processing of a benefit claim. The plaintiff, who was disabled with a back injury, sought to recover damages after her employer's disability committee terminated (and later reinstated) her disability benefits. The Court rejected the beneficiary's claim, explaining that ERISA Section 409 did not authorize a beneficiary to bring a claim against a fiduciary for monetary damages.[185] Based on the text of Section 409 and the legislative history of ERISA, the court opined that relief for an individual beneficiary was not available under Section 409; a plaintiff could only recover losses on behalf of the plan.

The Supreme Court's 2008 decision in *LaRue v. DeWolff, Boberg & Associates* addressed whether Section 502(a)(2) authorizes a participant in a defined contribution plan to sue a plan fiduciary and recover losses to the plan, if the losses only affected an individual's plan account.[186] In *LaRue*, a participant in a 401(k) plan requested that plan administrators change an investment in his individual account. The plan administrators failed to make this change, and the individual's account suffered losses of approximately $150,000. LaRue brought an action under Section 502(a)(2) alleging that the plan administrator breached his fiduciary duty by neglecting to properly follow the investment instructions. The Court held for the plan participant, finding that "although §502(a)(2) does not provide a remedy for individual injuries distinct from plan injuries, that provision does authorize recovery for fiduciary breaches that impair the value of plan assets in a participant's individual account." In the decision, Justice Stevens, writing for the majority, distinguished *LaRue* from the *Russell* case in two ways. First, the Court explained that the type of fiduciary misconduct occurring in *La Rue* violated "principal statutory duties" imposed by ERISA that "relate to the proper plan management, administration, and investment of fund assets."[187] Conversely, in *Russell*, the fiduciary's breach (*i.e.*, a delay in processing a benefit claim) fell outside of these principal duties.[188]

Second, the Court found that in *Russell,* the emphasis placed on protecting the "entire plan" from fiduciary breach under Section 409 applies to defined benefit plans, which were the norm at the time of the case.[189] However, as the Supreme Court noted in *LaRue*, defined contribution plans are more popular today, and the "entire plan" language in *Russell* does not apply to these plans. The Court explained that for defined benefit plans, fiduciary misconduct would not affect an individual entitlement to a benefit unless the misconduct detrimentally affected the entire plan. By contrast, "for defined contribution plans ... fiduciary misconduct need not threaten the solvency of the entire plan to reduce benefits below the amount that participants would otherwise receive."[190] The Court went on to note that "whether a fiduciary breach diminishes plan assets payable to all participants and beneficiaries, or only to persons tied to particular individual accounts, it creates the kinds of harms that concerned the draftsmen of §409."[191]

4. Claims to Enforce Plan Provisions and "Other Equitable Relief"

Section 502(a)(3) of ERISA permits a participant, beneficiary, or fiduciary, to bring a civil action to enjoin any act or practice which violates ERISA or the terms of the plan, or obtain "other appropriate equitable relief"[192] due to an ERISA violation. Section 502(a)(3) of ERISA has been referred to as a "catchall" provision — claims that may not be brought under other Sections of 502, but are nevertheless violations of ERISA or the plan, can be brought under this section.[193] The Supreme Court in *Varity v. Howe* found that individual relief under Section 502(a)(3) is available.[194] However, courts have struggled with the scope and meaning of the term "other appropriate equitable relief"in Section 502(a)(3). This issue has been considered one of the most controversial areas of ERISA jurisprudence.[195] The controversy has often arisen in cases in which plaintiffs had sought monetary relief for ERISA Section 502(a)(3) violations.

The Supreme Court first evaluated the meaning of "equitable relief" in *Mertens v. Hewitt Associates*.[196] In this case, plan participants brought an action under Section 502(a)(3) seeking monetary relief after the plan actuary failed to make proper actuarial assumptions in calculating plan assets. Participants claimed that this error contributed to plan underfunding, and subsequently, to the plan's defaulting on promised retirement benefits. The Court found that the monetary relief the participants sought was nothing other than compensatory damages, and held, in a 5-4 decision, that ERISA Section 502(a)(3) did not authorize suits for compensatory damages against a non-fiduciary. In explaining why these damages were not available, the Court articulated that "equitable relief" with respect to Section 502(a)(3) is relief that was "typically available in equity," such as injunction, mandamus, or restitution. While it had been argued that the relief petitioner sought was considered equitable under the common law of trusts, the Court rejected this argument. It explained that while "legal" remedies may have been available to plaintiffs in a court of equity, this idea did not "define the reach" of Section 502(a)(3), and that what was available under Section 502(a)(3) were the more "traditional" forms of equitable relief.[197]

The Supreme Court applied the reasoning of *Mertens* in another decision interpreting Section 502(a)(3), *Great West Life & Annuity Insurance Co. v. Knudson.*[198] In this case, a group health plan sought reimbursement from a plan beneficiary for amounts the plan had paid after the beneficiary was severely injured in an automobile accident. After the accident, the beneficiary brought an action against the automobile manufacturer and others, and she received a settlement. The plan claimed it was entitled to the settlement amount based on a provision in the plan requiring plan participants to reimburse the plan for any amounts the beneficiary receives from a third party.[199]

In another 5-4 decision, the Court found for the beneficiary, holding that Section 502(a)(3) did not authorize the reimbursement sought by the plan. The health plan claimed the relief sought was restitution,[200] which could be characterized as equitable relief. The Court refused to accept this reasoning, explaining that while restitution could be found traditionally in courts of equity, what mattered for purposes of Section 502(a)(3) was whether the restitution sought was to restore to the plaintiff particular funds or property in the defendant's possession. Because the proceeds of the settlement were not in the identifiable defendant's possession (i.e., they had been paid to a trust, to the plaintiff's attorney, etc.), the plaintiff's claim for equitable relief failed.[201]

5. Criminal Enforcement under ERISA and Other Federal Law

ERISA provides for three types of criminal sanctions. First, Section 501 provides that any person who willfully violates the reporting, disclosure and other related provisions[202] of ERISA may be fined up to $100,000, imprisoned up to 10 years, or both.[203] Persons other than individuals (*e.g.*, corporate entities) may be fined up to $500,000. Conduct that may be prosecuted under Section 501 includes a willful act as well as an omission to perform reporting or disclosure required by ERISA.[204] Second, Section 511 states that it is unlawful for any person to use (or threaten to use) fraud, force, or violence in interfering or preventing a person from exercising rights under an employee benefit plan.[205] Persons who willfully violate this section can be fined $100,000 or imprisoned for not more than ten years, or both.

Third, Section 411 bars individuals convicted of various crimes from holding certain positions with regard to an employee benefit plan.[206] Individuals convicted of these crimes may not serve (1) as an administrator, fiduciary, officer, trustee, custodian, counsel, agent, employee, or representative of a plan in any capacity; (2) as a consultant or advisor to a plan; or (3) in any capacity that involves decision- making authority or custody or control of the moneys, funds, assets or property of any plan.[207] Under this section, individuals may be barred from service during or for the period of 13 years after conviction or after imprisonment, whichever is later. This time period is subject to certain exceptions.[208] In addition, Section 411 prohibits an individual from knowingly hiring, retaining, employing, or otherwise placing someone to serve in any capacity which violates this section. Individuals who intentionally violate this provision are subject to a fine of no more than $10,000, up to five years imprisonment, or both.

Besides the three provisions under ERISA, the Federal Criminal Code prohibits certain conduct relating to employee benefit plans. Provisions under the Federal Criminal Code include the following:

Under Section 664 of Title 18, any person who embezzles, steals, or unlawfully and willfully abstracts or converts to his own use (or to the use of another) any assets of an employee benefit plan, will be fined, imprisoned no more than five years, or both. Assets of a plan include money, securities, premiums, and property.

Under Section 1127 of Title 18 of the United States Code, any individual who knowingly makes a false statement or representation of fact, or knowingly conceals, covers up, or fails to disclose any fact on certain documents required under ERISA may be subject to criminal penalties of up to $10,000, five years in prison, or both.

Section 1954 of Title 18 prohibits various persons serving in positions relating to employee benefit plans from (1) soliciting or receiving or (2) giving or offering any fee, kickback, commission, gift, loan, money or other item of value because of, or to influence, a certain question or matter concerning an employee benefit plan.[209] Persons violating this section may be fined, imprisoned for up to three years, or both. An exception to Section 1954 may be made for a person's salary, compensation, or other payments made for goods and services furnished or performed in the regular course of a person's duties to the plan.

Section 506(b) of ERISA provides that the Secretary of Labor has the responsibility and authority to detect, investigate, and refer both civil and criminal violations of ERISA as well as other related federal laws, including the provisions under the United States Criminal Code.[210] ERISA also requires the Secretary of Labor to provide evidence of crimes to the United States Attorney General, who may consider this evidence for purposes of criminal prosecution.[211]

K. Preemption of State Laws

A critical feature of ERISA is its preemption of state laws. According to the Supreme Court, Congress provided for ERISA preemption in order to "avoid a multiplicity of regulation in order to permit the nationally uniform administration of employee benefit plans."[212] ERISA preemption reflects this objective of ERISA: to regulate employee benefit plans "as exclusively a federal concern."[213]

The question of whether ERISA preempts state law has, at times, been complex and controversial. The provisions at issue in the preemption debate are (1) Section 514, ERISA's express preemption section, under which ERISA may supercede state law, and (2) Section 502(a), which provides for claims that may be brought and remedies a plaintiff may recover under ERISA, and may preempt a state law cause of action.

1. Section 514

ERISA's express preemption provision, Section 514, has three important parts.[214] First, under Section 514(a), ERISA preempts "any and all State laws insofar as they may now or hereafter relate to any employee benefit plan...." The Supreme Court has examined the scope of this provision on several occasions. In one of the first key cases to address ERISA preemption, *Shaw v. Delta Airlines*,[215] the Court interpreted the term "relate to" as applying to any state law that "has a connection with or reference to such a plan."[216] The Court has stated that "[u]nder this 'broad common sense meaning,' a state law may 'relate to' a benefit plan, and thereby be pre-empted, even if the law is not specifically designed to affect such plans, or the effect is only indirect."[217] While the Court's early decisions (*e.g.*, *Shaw*) suggested that the application of

ERISA's explicit preemption clause was virtually limitless, its decision in *New York State Conference of Blue Cross & Blue Shield Plans v. Travelers Insurance Co.* signaled a change in the Court's interpretation of Section 514(a).[218]

In *Travelers*, several commercial insurers challenged a state law that required them, but not Blue Cross and Blue Shield, to pay surcharges. The commercial insurers argued that the law was preempted by ERISA because it "relate[d] to" employer-sponsored health insurance plans. In addressing the issue of ERISA's preemption clause, the Court first noted that there is a "presumption that Congress does not intend to supplant state law."[219] The Court then turned to whether Congress intended to preempt state law by looking to "the structure and purpose of the act."[220] The Court concluded that "nothing in the language of the act or the context of its passage indicates that Congress chose to displace general health care regulation, which historically has been a matter of local concern."[221] In other cases, the Court has similarly recognized the states' ability to regulate matters of health and safety, and has concluded that state laws of general applicability are not necessarily preempted by ERISA.[222] However, despite the *Traveler*s case arguably narrowing the scope of Section 514(a), this section still is considered to broadly preempt state law.[223]

The second important part is the "savings clause" under ERISA Section 514(b), which provides exemptions to ERISA preemption. The savings clause allows states to enforce any "law ... which regulates insurance, banking, or securities."[224] The issue of which state laws "regulate insurance" under Section 514(b) has received considerable attention from the Supreme Court. An important case interpreting the savings clause is *Kentucky Association of Health Plans, Inc. v. Miller,*[225] where the Supreme Court found that Kentucky's "any willing provider" (AWP) laws, which prohibited insurers from discriminating against a health care provider willing to meet the insurer's criteria for participation in the health plan, was saved from ERISA preemption. In finding that the AWP laws "regulated insurance," the Court departed from reasoning it had used in earlier savings clause cases, and articulated a new two- part test.[226] Under this test, a state law falls within the ambit of the savings clause if it is "specifically directed toward" the insurance industry and "substantially affects the risk pooling arrangement between the insurer and insured."[227]

In evaluating whether the law was specifically directed toward the practice of insurance, the Court explained that the savings clause regulates *insurance*, not insurers, and that insurers may only be regulated "with respect to their insurance practices.[228] Petitioner HMOs argued, among other things, that the AWP laws were not directed toward insurers, as the laws regulated both the insurance industry and doctors who seek to form and maintain provider networks. The Court rejected this argument and pointed out that the law did not impose any prohibitions or requirements on health providers, and that health care providers were still able to enter into exclusive health care networks outside the state.

In regard to the second part of the new test, the Court explained that it was necessary for a law to affect the risk pooling arrangement between the insurer and the insured to be covered under the savings clause; otherwise, any law imposed upon an insurance company could be deemed to "regulate insurance."[229] Petitioners had argued that the AWP laws do not alter or affect the terms of insurance policies, but instead concern the relationship between insureds and third-party providers.[230] The Court disagreed and pointed out that it had never held that a state law must alter or control the terms of the insurance policies in order to "regulate insurance."[231] The Court found that AWP laws affected the risk pooling arrangement because they altered the scope of permissible bargains between insurers and insureds, and restricted insurers' ability to offer lower premiums in exchange for acceptance of a closed network of providers.[232]

The third important part of ERISA preemption, known as the "deemer clause," generally provides that an employee benefit plan governed by ERISA shall not be "deemed" an insurer, bank, trust company, investment company, or a company engaged in the insurance or banking business in order to be subject to state law (and accordingly, avoid ERISA preemption).[233] In *FMC v. Holliday*, the Supreme Court found that a Pennsylvania law that prevented subrogation[234] when applied to a self- funded health plan[235] was preempted by ERISA by virtue of the deemer clause. In its decision, the Court held that although the statute did "relate to" an ERISA benefit plan, the law fell within the ambit of the savings clause because the law controlled the terms of insurance contracts by invalidating any subrogation provisions that they contain.[236] However, because the plan in question was a self-funded plan (*i.e.,* it did not offer benefits through health insurance), it was found that the plan could not be "deemed" an insured plan for the purpose of state regulation.

2. Section 502

ERISA preemption can also be found in ERISA's remedial provisions under Section 502. Section 502(a) creates a civil enforcement scheme that allows a participant or beneficiary of a plan to bring a civil action for various reasons, including "to recover benefits due to him under the terms of the plan, to enforce his rights under the terms of the plan, or to clarify his rights to future benefits under the terms of the plan." If a plaintiff seeks to bring a state law claim is "within the scope" of Section 5 02(a), the state law claim can be preempted.[237] See the "Administration and Enforcement" section of this chapter for additional discussion of ERISA Section 502.

L. Special Regulation of Health Benefits

Besides the regulation of pension plans, ERISA also regulates welfare benefit plans[238] offered by an employer to provide medical, surgical and other health benefits. ERISA applies to health benefit coverage offered through health insurance or other arrangements (*e.g.*, self-funded plans).

Health plans, like other welfare benefit plans governed by ERISA, must comply with certain standards, including plan fiduciary standards, reporting and disclosure requirements, and procedures for appealing a denied claim for benefits. However, these health plans must also meet additional requirements under ERISA. As enacted in 1974, ERISA's regulation of health plan coverage and benefits was limited. However, beginning in 1986, Congress added to ERISA a number of requirements on the nature and content of health plans, including rules governing health care continuation coverage, limitations on exclusions from coverage based on preexisting conditions, parity between medical/surgical benefits and mental health benefits, and minimum hospital stay requirements for mothers following the birth of a child.[239]

1. COBRA

The *Consolidated Omnibus Budget Reconciliation Act of 1985* (COBRA) added a new Part 6 to Title I of ERISA, which requires the sponsor of a group health plan to provide an option of temporarily continuing health care coverage for plan participants and beneficiaries under certain circumstances.[240] Under ERISA Section 601, a plan maintained by an employer with 20 or more employees must provide "qualified beneficiaries"[241] with the option of continuing coverage under the employer's group health plan in the case of certain "qualified events." A qualifying event is an event that, except for continuation coverage under COBRA, would result in a loss of coverage, such as the death of the covered employee, the termination (other than by reason of the employee's gross misconduct) or reduction of hours of the covered employee's employment, or the covered employee becoming entitled to Medicare benefits.[242]

Under Section 602 of ERISA, the employer must typically provide this continuation coverage for 18 months.[243] However, coverage may be longer, depending on the qualifying event.[244] Under ERISA 602(1), the benefits offered under COBRA must be identical to the health benefits offered to "similarly situated non-COBRA beneficiaries," or in other words, beneficiaries who have not experienced a qualifying event. The health plan may charge a premium to COBRA participants, but it cannot exceed 102% of the plan's group rate. After 18 months of required coverage, a plan may charge certain participants 150% of the plan's group rate.

2. HIPAA

The *Health Insurance Portability and Accountability Act of 1996* (HIPAA) added a new Part 7 to Title I of ERISA to provide additional health plan coverage requirements.[245] Other federal legislation amended Part 7 of ERISA to require plans to offer specific health benefits. The requirements of Part 7 generally apply to group health plans, as well as "health insurance issuers"[246] that offer group health insurance coverage.[247] HIPAA amended ERISA to limit the circumstances under which a health plan may exclude a participant or beneficiary with a preexisting condition from coverage.[248] This exclusion from coverage cannot be for more than 12 months after an employee enrolls in a health plan (or 18 months for late enrollees). HIPAA prohibits pre-existing condition coverage exclusions for any conditions relating to pregnancy. Similarly, newborns and adopted children may not be excluded from plan enrollment if they were covered under "creditable coverage" within 30 days after birth or adoption, and there has not been a gap of more than 64 days in this coverage.[249]

HIPAA also created ERISA Section 702, which provides that a group health plan or health insurance issuer may not base coverage[250] eligibility rules on certain health-related factors, such as medical history or disability.[251] In addition, a health plan may not require an individual to pay a higher premium or contribution than another "similarly situated" participant, based on these health-related factors.[252] HIPAA also added Section 703 of ERISA, which provides that certain health plans covering multiple employers cannot deny an employer (whose employees are covered by the plan) coverage under the plan, except for certain reasons, such as an employer's failure to pay plan contributions.[253]

3. Mental Health Parity

In 1996, Congress enacted the *Mental Health Parity Act* (MHPA), which added Section 712 of ERISA to create certain requirements for mental health coverage, if this coverage was offered by a health plan.[254] Under the MHPA, health plans are not required to offer mental health benefits. However, plans that choose to provide mental health benefits must not impose lower annual and lifetime dollar limits on these benefits than the limits placed on medical and surgical benefits. The MHPA allows a plan to decide what mental health benefits are to be offered; however, the parity requirements do not apply to substance abuse or chemical dependency treatment.[255]

Certain plans may be exempt from the MHPA. Plans covering employers with 50 or fewer employees are exempt from compliance. In addition, employers that experience an increase in claims costs of at least 1% as a result of MHPA compliance can apply for an exemption. The MHPA was authorized through December 31, 2007. However, recent efforts have been made to extend these provisions though December 31, 2008.[256]

4. Maternity Length of Stay

In 1996, Congress passed the *Newborns' and Mothers' Health Protection Act* (NMHPA), which amended ERISA and established minimum hospital stay requirements for mothers following the birth of a child.[257] In general, the NMHPA prohibits a group health plan or health insurance issuer from limiting a hospital length of stay in connection with childbirth for the mother or newborn child to less than 48 hours, following a normal vaginal delivery,[258] and to less than 96 hours, following a cesarean section.[259]

5. Reconstructive Surgery Following Mastectomies

The *Women's Health and Cancer Rights Act*, enacted in 1998, amended ERISA to require group health plans providing mastectomy coverage to cover prosthetic devices and reconstructive surgery.[260] Under Section 713 of ERISA, this coverage must be provided in a manner determined in consultation between the attending physician and the patient.[261]

ERISA Title II. Internal Revenue Code Provisions

In order for an employer-sponsored retirement plan to qualify for federal income tax deferrals and deductions, it must comply with the pension-related provisions of the Internal Revenue Code (IRC). The pension-related provisions of the IRC require plans to cover rank-and-file workers, and they include "nondiscrimination rules" that prohibit qualified plans from favoring highly-compensated employees with respect to eligibility or benefits.[262]

A. Limits on Plan Contributions and Benefits

The IRC limits the amount of money that can be contributed on a tax-deductible basis to a defined benefit plan or defined contribution plan, the amount that can be paid annually from a defined benefit plan, and the amount of income that can be taken into consideration when establishing benefits under a defined benefit plan.

1. Defined Benefit Plan Provisions

In 2008, no more than the first $230,000 of an employee's annual compensation can be used in computing benefits or contributions under a DB plan.[263] The maximum annual benefit payable in 2008 under a defined benefit plan at age 62 is the lesser of $185,000 or 100% percent of the participant's average compensation for his or her three highest years of earnings.[264] This dollar limit is adjusted annually by the increase in the consumer price index (CPI), and rounded down to the next lower multiple of $5,000. IRC §415(b) requires the dollar limit on benefits to be actuarially reduced for retirement before age 62. For qualified police and firefighters with at least 15 years of service, no actuarial reduction is required. Consequently, the dollar limit for police and firefighters is the same as the unreduced §415(b) dollar limit, or $185,000 in 2008, regardless of age.

a. Tax on Asset Reversions

ERISA prohibits plan sponsors from withdrawing money from a pension trust fund. However, they can recover "excess" assets upon terminating a plan, provided they have satisfied all pension claims. The employer must pay both a corporate income tax and a federal excise tax on the amount of the asset reversion. The *Omnibus Budget Reconciliation Act of 1990* (P.L. 101-508) amended the IRC to increase the excise tax on pension asset reversions from 15% to 50%, unless the employer: (1) establishes or maintains a "qualified replacement plan;" (2) provides significant benefit increases; or (3) is in bankruptcy liquidation.[265] In these cases, the excise tax is 20%. A qualified replacement plan must cover at least 95% of the active participants in the terminated plan, and 25% of the amount the employer could otherwise receive in a reversion must be transferred to the replacement plan.[266] The amount transferred is not subject to the excise tax or corporate income tax.

b. Transfers of Assets to Fund Retiree Health Benefits

P.L. 101-508 permitted the transfer of excess assets from a single-employer defined benefit pension plan to a retiree health plan.[267] The amount that could be transferred was the excess of the market value of the plan's assets over the full funding limit, but could not exceed what the employer expected to pay in retiree health benefits in that year. Transfers were limited to the greater of amounts above the plan's full-funding limit or 125% of the plan's current liability. The PPA amended IRC §420 to expand the ability of defined benefit plan sponsors to transfer surplus plan assets to retiree health plans. Sponsors of single-employer plans may now transfer excess pension assets to fund the estimated retiree medical costs for a period of up to 10 years. Plan sponsors are required to maintain the plan's funded status during the transfer period, either by additional contributions or transfers back from the health accounts, and they must maintain retiree medical benefits at a certain level for the transfer period and for four years subsequent to the transfer period.

c. Limit on Tax Deductions for Employer Contributions

In 2007, the maximum tax-deductible employer contribution to a defined benefit plan was 150% of the plan's current liability minus the value of the plan's assets. Beginning in 2008, the maximum tax-deductible employer contribution is (1) the plan's target normal cost plus (2) 150% of the funding target plus (3) an allowance for future pay or benefit increases minus (4) the value of the plan's assets.[268] Excess employer contributions to defined benefit plans are subject to a 10% excise tax.

2. Defined Contribution Plan Provisions

IRC §415(c) limits the maximum "annual addition" to a defined contribution plan (the sum of employer and employee contributions). In 2008, the maximum annual addition is the lesser of $46,000 or 100% of annual compensation.[269] The maximum employee contribution (called an "elective deferral") to a 401(k), 403(b), or 457(b) plan is $15,500 in 2008.[270] This amount is indexed annually in $500 increments.

a. Combined Limit under IRC §404 (a)(7)

IRC §404(a)(7) establishes limits on employer tax deductions for contributions made in connection with one or more defined contribution plans *and* one or more defined benefit plans. One effect of these limits is that large contributions to a defined benefit plan could result in the employer's contributions to the defined contribution plan being nondeductible for that year. The PPA revised the law such that the combined contribution limit under §404(a)(7) is determined without regard to defined benefit plans that are insured by the PBGC. In addition, only employer contributions to a defined contribution plan that exceed 6% of participant compensation are subject to the limit. Employees' elective deferrals are disregarded from the deduction limits.

b. "Catch-Up" Contributions

The *Economic Growth and Tax Relief Reconciliation Act of 2001*[271] added §414(v) to the Internal Revenue Code. This amendment allows additional ("catch-up") contributions by participants in 401(k), 403(b), 457(b), SEP, IRA, and SIMPLE plans who are or will be age 50 or older by the end of the plan year. These contributions were to "sunset" in 2010, but they were made permanent by the PPA. The maximum catch-up contribution is the lesser of (1) a specific dollar limit or (2) the participant's compensation for the year reduced by any other elective deferrals made during the year. In 2008, the catch-up dollar limit for 401(k), 403(b), SEP, and 457(b) plans is $5,000. For SIMPLE plans, the 2008 catch-up dollar limit is $2,500. For IRAs, the catch-up dollar limit is $1,000.

B. Coverage and Nondiscrimination

Tax-qualified retirement plans may not discriminate in favor of *highly-compensated employees* (HCEs) with regard to coverage, amount of benefits, or availability of benefits.[272] A "highly compensated employee" is defined in law as any employee who owns 5% or more of the company or whose compensation in 2008 exceeds $105,000 (indexed to inflation).[273] An employer can elect to count as HCEs only employees who rank in the top 20% of compensation in the firm, but must include anyone who owns 5% or more of the company.

1. Nondiscrimination Test

IRC §410(b) specifies who a qualified plan must cover. A plan must meet one of the following tests:

The plan must benefit at least 70% of non-highly compensated employees. This is called the percentage test.

or

The plan must benefit a percentage of nonhighly compensated employees which is at least 70% of the percentage of highly compensated employees benefitting under the plan. This is called the ratio test.

or

The plan must benefit a classification of employees that does not discriminate in favor of highly-compensated employees (nondiscriminatory classification test) and the average benefit percentage of the nonhighly compensated employees must be at least 70% of the average benefit percentage of the highly-compensated employees (average benefit percentage test).

In a defined contribution plan, either the proportion of non-highly compensated employees (NHCEs) covered by the plan must be at least 70% of the proportion of highly compensated employees (HCEs) covered by the plan, or the average contribution percentage for NHCEs must be at least 70% of the average contribution percentage for HCEs.[274] Plans that have after-tax contributions or matching contributions are subject to the "actual contribution percentage" (ACP) test, which measures the contribution rate to HCEs' accounts relative to the contribution rate to NHCEs' accounts. Some §403(b) plans are subject to nondiscrimination rules; §457 plans generally are not. The actual contribution percentage of HCEs in a §401(k) plan generally cannot exceed the limits shown in **Table 2**.

2. Safe Harbor Plans

Any of three "safe-harbor" 401(k) plan designs are deemed to satisfy the ACP test automatically for employer matching contributions (up to 6% of compensation):

The employer matches 100% of employee elective deferrals up to 3% of compensation, and 50% of elective deferrals between 3% and 5% of compensation, and all employer matching contributions vest immediately.

Employer matching contributions can follow any other matching formula that results in total matching contributions that are no less than under the first design. All employer matching contributions must vest immediately.

Table 2. Maximum Average 401(k) Contributions for Highly Compensated Employees

Nonhighly compensated employees (NHCEs)	Highly compensated employees (HCEs)
Maximum average deferral and match:	*Maximum average deferral and match:*
2% of pay or less	NHCE percentage X 2
More than 2% and less than 8% of pay	NHCE percentage + 2%
8% of pay or more	NHCE percentage X 1.25

Note: "Deferral and match" is the sum of employer and employee contributions.

The employer automatically contributes an amount equal to at least 3% of pay for all eligible NHCEs. Employer contributions must vest immediately.

All 401(k) plans must satisfy an "actual deferral percentage" (ADP) test, which measures employees' elective deferrals. The same numerical limits are used as under the ACP test. Three "safe-harbor" designs, similar to the safe-harbor designs for the ACP test, are deemed to satisfy the ADP test automatically. In addition, "cross-testing" allows defined-contribution plans to satisfy the nondiscrimination tests based on projected account balances at retirement age, rather than current contribution rates. This permits bigger contributions for older workers. Because higher-paid employees receive proportionally smaller Social Security benefits relative to earnings than lower-paid workers, employers are permitted to make larger contributions on earnings in excess of the Social Security wage base ($102,000 in 2008). Regulations limit the size of the *permitted disparity* in favor of workers whose earnings are above the wage base.

C. Distributions from Qualified Plans

The *Tax Reform Act of 1986*[275] created uniform distribution rules for pension plans and established an excise tax to be imposed for failure to make a required minimum distribution. This law also specified that, if there were *after-tax* employee contributions to a plan, a portion of each payment to the participant is to be considered a return of employee contributions (and not taxed) and that a portion is to be considered a return of employer contributions (and subject to tax). Defined benefit plans and money purchase plans must offer participants a benefit in the form of a life annuity. Defined benefit and money purchase plans may also offer other payment options, such as lump-sum distributions. Defined contribution plans other than money purchase plans usually pay benefits in a single lump-sum or as payments over a set period of time, such as 5 or 10 years. Some of these plans also offer an annuity option.

A qualified plan must allow participants to begin receiving benefits by the latest of (1) age 65 (or the plan's normal retirement age, if earlier than 65), or (2) after ten years of service, or (3) upon terminating service with the employer.[276] Defined benefit plans and money purchase plans usually allow participants to receive benefits only after they have reached the plan's normal retirement age, but some have provisions for early retirement, often at age 55. Most 401(k) plans allow participants to receive their account balances when they leave the employer. A 401(k) plan may allow for distributions while the worker is still employed if he or she has reached age 59½ or has suffered a severe financial hardship, such as facing imminent eviction or foreclosure. Profit-sharing plans may permit participants to receive their vested benefits after a specific number of years or when they leave the employer.

Distributions from employer-sponsored plans must start no later than April 1 of the year after the year in which the participant attains age 70½, unless the participant is still employed by the form that sponsors the plan.[277] Failure to make a required distribution results in an excise tax equal to 50% of the excess of the minimum required distribution over the amount actually distributed. The amount of the required minimum distribution is based on the participant's age and remaining life expectancy. If a participant in a DB plan retires after age 70½, his or her accrued pension benefit must be actuarially increased to reflect the value of benefits that would have been received had the employee retired at age 70½. The actuarial adjustment rule does not apply to defined contribution plans.

Some employers now offer a "phased retirement" option that allows employees at or near retirement age to reduce their work hours to part-time and receive a pension distribution to supplement their reduced earnings. The PPA amended ERISA to allow defined benefit plans to make in-service distributions to employed plan participants beginning at the earlier of age 62 or the plan's normal retirement age.[278] Distributions from a 401(k) plan can be made to a current employee without penalty beginning at age 59½.[279] In-service distributions from either a DB plan or a DC plan are subject to income taxes.

1. Plan Loans

Qualified plans are permitted, but are not required, to offer loans to participants. The loan must charge a reasonable rate of interest and be adequately secured. A loan from a tax-qualified pension plan is treated for federal income tax purposes as a taxable plan distribution if it exceeds prescribed limits.[280] The maximum permissible loan amount takes into account other outstanding plan loans as well as the present value of the benefits earned by the recipient. A participant can borrow up to half of the present value of accrued benefits, but no more than $50,000. The loan must be repaid within five years unless it is used to purchase a principal residence. Loans that are not repaid when due are treated as taxable distributions and may also be subject to a 10% additional tax if the recipient was under age 59½. Defined contribution plans established under §401(k), §403(b), or §457 also can make distributions in case of financial hardship, such as imminent eviction or foreclosure. Hardship distributions are subject to income taxes, and if the recipient is under age 59½, they may be subject to an additional 10% tax.

2. Additional Tax on Early Withdrawals

With certain exceptions, a 10% additional tax is imposed on distributions from a qualified plan unless the individual is age 59½, dies, or becomes disabled.[281] This additional tax does not apply to early distributions if they are paid:

(1) after the plan participant has reached age 59½;
(2) to a beneficiary after the death of the participant;
(3) because the participant has become disabled;
(4) as part of a series of *substantially equal periodic payments* (SEPPs) over the life of the participant or the joint lives of the participant and survivor;
(5) to an employee who has separated from service under an early retirement arrangement after reaching age 55;[282]

(6) as dividends paid from an Employee Stock Ownership Plan (ESOP);
(7) through an IRS levy to collect back taxes owed by the plan participant;
(8) to pay medical expenses of the plan participant, a spouse, or dependent, but only to the extent that they exceed 7.5% of adjusted gross income; or
(9) to an alternate payee under a qualified domestic relations order (QDRO).

3. Rollovers

Departing plan participants can roll over (transfer) distributions from a qualified plan to an individual retirement account (IRA) or to another employer's plan, if the plan accepts such transfers. If the accrued benefit is less than $5,000 when the participant leaves an employer, the plan can make an immediate distribution without the participant's consent. Amounts of $5,000 or more may be cashed out only with the written consent of the participant. For married workers, the consent of the worker's spouse is also required.

If the distribution is more than $1,000, the plan must automatically roll over the funds into an IRA that it selects, unless the participant elects to receive a lump sum payment or to roll it over into an IRA that he or she chooses. The plan must first send a notice allowing the participant to make other arrangements, and it must follow rules regarding what type of IRA can be used (for example, it cannot combine the distribution with savings the individual has deposited directly in an IRA). Rollovers must be made to an entity that is qualified to offer individual retirement plans. Also, the rollover IRA must have investments designed to preserve principal. The IRA provider may not charge more in fees and expenses for such plans than it would to its other IRA customers.

If the departing employee elects to receive a lump sum payment and does not transfer the money to another qualified employer plan or to an IRA, the participant will owe a 10% tax penalty if he or she is under age 591/2 and does not meet the exceptions listed in §72(t). Distributions paid directly to the plan participant rather than being rolled over into an IRA or a qualified employer plan are subject to mandatory tax withholding equal to 20% of the total distribution. If the rollover — which must be equal to the cash received *plus* the 20% withheld — is completed within 60 days of the distribution, the tax that was withheld is applied to the individual's income tax liability.

D. Integration with Social Security

The Social Security benefit formula is designed to replace a greater percentage of wages for lower-income workers than for higher-income workers. The Social Security Administration estimates that for benefits claimed at the full retirement age, Social Security currently replaces 55% of the average earnings of a low-wage worker and 27% of the earnings of a high-wage worker.[283] Since the *Revenue Act of 1942*, it has been permissible for private pension plans to narrow the difference in total wage replacement by providing larger pension benefits as a percentage of compensation to higher-paid workers than to lower-paid workers. Plans may coordinate or "integrate" their retirement benefit formulas with Social Security under an "offset method" or an "excess method."[284]

In defined benefit plans, integration with Social Security is usually related to the *benefit paid* to participants, while in defined contribution plans it most often relates to the *contributions made* by employers. In an integrated defined benefit plan, the amount of the worker's monthly pension is reduced or "offset" by a percentage of his or her Social Security benefit. In an integrated defined contribution plan, the amount contributed by the employer is higher for the portion of the employee's salary that is *in excess* of a specific amount, called the integration level. The most common integration level is the maximum amount of annual income that is subject to Social Security taxes ($102,000 in 2008). The maximum offset allowed under an offset plan and the "maximum permitted disparity" allowed under an excess plan are both limited by the tax code.

E. Special Rules for "Top-heavy" Plans

A defined benefit pension plan is considered "top-heavy" if more than 60% of benefits (in a DB plan) are earned by key employees or if more than 60% of contributions (in a DC plan) are made on behalf of key employees.[285] Key employees are defined as company officers with earnings over $150,000 in 2008, owners of at least 1% of the company who receive over $150,000 in annual compensation, and owners of 5% or more of the company. For any plan year in which a plan is found to be top-heavy, special requirements must be met if the plan is to retain its tax-qualified status. Top-heavy plan requirements fall into two main areas: (1) faster vesting schedules for non-key employees;

and (2) minimum nonintegrated benefits and contributions for non-key employees.

Top-heavy plans must implement an accelerated vesting schedule. The benefits vested must include all benefits accrued (earned) under the plan, not just those accrued while the plan is operating under the special top-heavy rules. Top-heavy plans may choose from one of two special vesting schedules. Under the first, plan participants must be 100% vested in their benefits after three years of service. Under the second, 100% vesting occurs after six years and is reached by stages: 20% of the employee's accrued benefits are vested after two years of service, and an additional 20% become vested after each of the next four years.

For years in which a plan is deemed to be top-heavy, the plan must meet specific minimum benefit and contribution levels for every non-key employee covered by the plan. The specified minimum benefit or contribution may not be reduced or eliminated through integration with Social Security. For each year that a defined benefit plan is top-heavy, a minimum benefit is required equal to 2% of the employee's average compensation earned for the five highest consecutive years of compensation. The highest minimum benefit does not have to exceed 20% of the non-key employee's average compensation. For each year that a defined contribution plan is top-heavy, the employer must make a contribution on behalf of each non-key employee equal to at least 3% of the employee's annual compensation.

ERISA Title III. Jurisdiction, Administration, and Enforcement

Title III of ERISA covers jurisdictional, administrative and enforcement matters.[286] Under this title, various enforcement and regulatory responsibilities are coordinated between the Department of Labor, the Treasury Department, and the Pension Benefit Guaranty Corporation (PBGC).

Under Section 3001 of ERISA, before the Treasury Department issues a determination letter regarding whether a plan has met certain requirements under the Internal Revenue Code, the Treasury Department must allow certain employees, as well as the Department of Labor and the PBGC, the opportunity to comment on the application. Section 3002 provides that if the Secretary of Labor or the PBGC want to bring a claim against a party for violation of the participation, vesting, or funding provisions of ERISA, the Secretary and the

PBGC must give the Secretary of the Treasury a reasonable opportunity to review the brief.[287] ERISA also gives the Secretary of the Treasury the right to intervene in these cases.

Section 3003 provides that unless collection of the tax is in jeopardy, the Secretary of the Treasury must notify the Secretary of Labor before sending a notice of deficiency relating to a tax imposed on a prohibited transaction.[288] The Secretary of the Treasury must also give the Secretary of Labor an opportunity to comment on the imposition of the tax.[289] Under Section 3004 of ERISA, whenever the Secretary of the Treasury and the Secretary of Labor are required to carry out provisions in ERISA (or a federal law amended by ERISA) that relate to the same subject matter, the Secretaries must consult with each other to develop rules, regulations, practices, and forms.[290] This collaboration is to encourage efficient administration of the provisions, and prevent duplication of efforts by the agencies, as well as creation of additional burden for plan administrators, employers, participants and beneficiaries.[291]

ERISA Title IV. Pension Benefit Guaranty Corporation and Plan Termination

Title IV of ERISA established the Pension Benefit Guaranty Corporation (PBGC) as a government-owned corporation to protect the retirement income of participants and beneficiaries in private-sector defined benefit pension plans. Defined contribution plans such as ESOPs, profit-sharing plans, 401(k), 403(b), thrift/savings plans, and stock bonus plans are not insured by the PBGC. The insurance program treats pension plans differently depending on whether they are single-employer plans or multiemployer plans (i.e., collectively bargained plans to which more than one company makes contributions). The PBGC maintains separate reserve funds for single-employer plans and multiemployer plans.

A. Premiums for Single-employer Plans

The PBGC receives no appropriations from Congress. Its revenues come from premiums paid by employers that sponsor defined benefit pension plans, the assets of the terminated plans that it has taken over, investment income on its trust funds, and amounts recovered from the general assets of firms that terminate underfunded pension plans. Although it receives no appropriations, the *Multiemployer Pension Plan Amendments Act of 1980* (P.L. 96-364) requires the PBGC's receipts and disbursements to be included in the federal budget. The PBGC does not have the legal authority to set its own premiums, which are set in law by Congress. The PBGC single-employer insurance program receives two types of premiums from plan sponsors: a per-capita premium that is charged to all single-employer defined benefit plans and a variable premium charged to underfunded plans. The *Deficit Reduction Act of 2005*[292] increased the per capita premium from $19 per year to $30 per year for single-employer plans and indexed future premiums to average national wage growth. The per-capita premium is $33 in 2008.

The variable premium is equal to $9 per $1,000 of underfunded vested benefits. The interest rate for determining the amount of underfunding subject to the variable rate premium is based on a composite corporate bond rate for the month preceding the month in which the premium payment year begins. Under prior law, an underfunded plan was exempted from the variable-rate premium if it was not underfunded in any two consecutive years out of the previous three years. Under the PPA, the variable premium is assessed on all underfunded plans, regardless of the plan's funding status in earlier years. For employers with 25 or fewer employees, the variable premium is $5 per participant.

The PPA made permanent a surcharge premium for certain distress terminations that was added by P.L. 109-171 and was to expire in 2010. An annual surcharge of $1,250 per participant will be assessed for three years against any firm that terminates an underfunded pension plan during bankruptcy if it later emerges from bankruptcy.

B. PBGC Insurance Limit

The PBGC guarantees only "basic benefits." Basic benefits include pension benefits beginning at normal retirement age (usually age 65), certain early retirement and disability benefits, and benefits for survivors of deceased plan participants.[293] Only vested benefits are insured. ERISA sets a limit on the benefits insured by the PBGC. This limit is adjusted annually for increases in wage growth in the economy. For pension plans ending in 2008, the maximum yearly pension guarantee is $51,750 for a participant retiring at age 65. The maximum insured benefit is reduced actuarially if a participant retires before age 65 or if the pension plan provides benefits in a form other than a life annuity.[294] Benefits are insured at their nominal value: once the insured benefit amount is determined, it is not adjusted for inflation. Benefit increases that went into effect less than five years before a plan was terminated are not fully insured. Insurance on these benefits is phased in, guaranteeing 20% of the increase in benefits for each full year since the amendment that increased plan benefits was adopted.

C. Plan Terminations[295]

A sponsor of a single-employer plan can voluntarily end the pension plan in one of two ways: (1) a "standard" termination if the plan is fully funded; or (2) a "distress" termination that allows a sponsor in serious financial trouble to terminate a plan that may be less than fully funded. In addition, the PBGC may terminate a plan involuntarily if certain conditions are met. The PBGC becomes responsible for paying benefits in the case of a distress or involuntary termination.

1. Standard Termination

An employer can end a plan through a standard termination only if the plan's assets are sufficient to cover all of the plan's liabilities. Participants and beneficiaries must be informed of the amounts due them, including the data and underlying actuarial assumptions used to compute the benefits. An actuary must certify that the assets are sufficient to meet all plan liabilities. If the rules for a standard termination have been met, the plan sponsor purchases annuities from a commercial insurer or distributes lump-sum payments to beneficiaries. The employer then has no further liability to the PBGC or plan participants and can recapture any remaining assets after paying all applicable taxes.

2. Distress Termination

An employer can terminate an underfunded plan under a distress termination only if one of the following conditions applies:

Bankruptcy proceedings seeking liquidation have been filed by or against the company under Chapter 7 of the Bankruptcy Code;

The company is undergoing reorganization under Chapter 11of the Code and the bankruptcy court has approved a plan termination;

The company is unable to pay its debts when due and will be unable to continue in business unless the plan is ended; or

The company has experienced unreasonably burdensome pension costs solely as a result of a decline in its workforce.

One of the criteria for a distress termination must be met by each company that is a contributing sponsor of the plan or a "substantial member" of the sponsor's controlled group. Generally, a substantial member is a company whose assets comprise 5% or more of the total assets of the controlled group. The controlled group includes corporate parents and affiliates of the plan sponsor.

3. Involuntary Termination

The PBGC may end a pension plan even if a company has not filed to do so on its own initiative. PBGC may end the plan if:

The plan has not met the minimum funding requirements;

The plan cannot pay current benefits when due;

A lump-sum payment has been made to a participant who is a substantial owner of the sponsoring company; or

The loss to the PBGC is expected to increase unreasonably if the plan is not ended.

D. Employer Liability to the PBGC[296]

In a distress termination, or in an involuntary termination initiated by the PBGC, a pension plan sponsor is liable to the PBGC for any unfunded benefit liabilities. The plan sponsor and members of the controlled group are jointly and severally liable for such obligation, so each member can be held responsible for the entire liability. Each contributing sponsor also would be liable to the PBGC if the plan had an accumulated funding deficiency or a waived funding deficiency. The employer liability to the PBGC is due on the termination date, except that the PBGC can prescribe commercially reasonable terms for payment of employer liability that exceeds 30 percent of the net worth of the employer. If a company sells or transfers a business with an underfunded pension plan for the purpose of evading pension liabilities and the plan is ended within five years of the sale or transfer, the firm can be held liable for unfunded liabilities existing at the time of sale.

E. Reportable Events

The PBGC must be notified of certain events, including: (1) if the plan is deemed not in compliance with the law; (2) if an amendment has been adopted decreasing benefits; (3) if there has been a substantial drop in the number of active participants; (4) if the plan does not meet the minimum funding standards or is unable to pay benefits; or (5) if there is a distribution of $10,000 or more to a substantial owner. The PBGC also must be notified if a controlled group member leaves the group, liquidates, declares an extraordinary dividend, or redeems 10% or more of total voting stock.

F. Notice Requirements

As amended by the PPA, ERISA requires that if a defined benefit plan terminates while it is underfunded through a distress termination under ERISA §4041(c), or is subject to an involuntary termination under ERISA §4042, the plan sponsor must provide to plan participants the same information that the plan is required to submit to the PBGC — subject to confidentiality limitations — within 15 days of the PBGC filing.[297] This requirement applies to notices of intent to terminate and involuntary termination determinations.

G. Premiums for Multiemployer Pension Plans[298]

Multiemployer pension plans were covered by PBGC insurance by the *Multiemployer Pension Plan Amendments Act of 1980* (P.L. 96-364). The rules for multiemployer plans differ from those applicable to single-employer plans because of the special nature of these arrangements. The PBGC is required to provide financial assistance to insolvent multiemployer plans, whether or not they are terminated, when the assistance is needed to enable the plan to pay guaranteed benefits. The PBGC guarantees 100% of the first $11 of monthly benefits earned per year of service plus 75% of the next $33 of monthly benefits per year of service. The 75% guarantee is reduced to 65% if the plan does not meet specified funding requirements. The annual insurance premium charged for each plan participant in a multiemployer plan is $9 in 2008 and is indexed to wage growth in future years.

H. Withdrawal Liability[299]

Employers who leave a multiemployer plan for any reason continue to be liable for a portion of any underfunding. The purpose of the withdrawal liability is to protect the remaining contributing employers and the PBGC from having to assume the burden of funding the pension obligations of employers who cease contributing to the plan. The withdrawal liability is imposed at the time of withdrawal and does not depend on the actual termination of the plan. This rule is designed to discourage withdrawals by requiring each employer to continue funding its share of the plan's unfunded vested liability. Withdrawal liability is equal to an employer's share of the plan's unfunded vested liability determined under one of several rules that may be adopted by the plan, and is payable to the plan in annual installments for a period of up to 20 years. An employer first entering a multiemployer plan is allowed a six-year "free look" during which it can participate in the plan without incurring withdrawal liability. This provision is not available if the employer would account for 2% or more of total contributions to the plan.

GLOSSARY

This glossary contains terms used within ERISA and the Internal Revenue Code. It also contains certain abbreviations used within this chapter.

Accrual of Benefits. In the case of a *defined benefit* pension plan, the process of accumulating pension credits for years of service, expressed in the form of an annual benefit that is first paid at normal retirement age (usually age 65). In the case of a *defined contribution* plan, the process of accumulating assets from contributions and investment earnings in an individual employee's plan account.

Accrual Rate. The benefit amount or percentage of pre-retirement salary earned for a year of service.

Accrued Liability. The present value of future benefits less the present value of the contributions for future *normal costs*, taking into consideration projected salary increases and future service.

Actuarial Liability. Actuarial cost methods generally divide the present value of future benefits into two parts: the part attributable to the past and the part attributable to the future. The part attributable to the past is called the *actuarial liability* while that attributable to the future is called the *present value of future normal costs*.

Actuarial Assumption. Assumptions about future economic and demographic developments related to the pension plan that are used by plan actuaries in calculating the annual pension contribution. There are two key actuarial assumptions for pension funds: the interest rate assumption and the salary assumption. The former is an assumption about the investment return likely to be earned by the assets of a pension fund over a long period of time. The latter is an estimate of how rapidly employee salaries will increase over the same period.

Actuarial Funding Method. The schedule of contributions to meet the plan's liabilities for benefit payments. There are several allowable funding methods, and each produces a different flow of contributions. Some produce increasing contributions, others level contributions, and still others declining contributions.

Amortization. Paying off a liability through a series of installments, including interest.

Annuity. (a) The specified monthly or annual payment to a pensioner, often used interchangeably with the term "pension;" (b) A contract that provides an income for a specified period of time, such as a number of years or for life; (c) The periodic payments provided under an annuity contract with a commercial insurance company.

Beneficiary. A person designated by a pension plan participant, or by the terms of an *employee benefit plan*, who is or may become entitled to a benefit under that plan (e.g., a spouse).

Cash Balance Plan. A cash balance plan is a defined benefit plan that defines the benefit in terms of a stated account balance. Cash balance plans are sometimes called hybrid plans because, while they are considered to be defined benefit plans, they are designed to look to participants much like defined contribution plans. The participant is credited with a percentage of pay each year in a hypothetical account on which the employer pays interest. These accounts, however, are merely accounting devices that track the worker's accrued benefit. They are not individual accounts owned by the participants, as they would be in a defined contribution plan. As a defined benefit plan, a cash balance plan must offer participants the option of receiving an annuity at retirement age. Most cash balance plans also offer separating employees a lump sum payment in lieu of an annuity.

Cash or Deferred Arrangement. See 401(k) plan.

Catch-up contributions. Additional contributions to IRAs and defined contributions by persons age 50 or older authorized by the E*conomic Growth and Tax Relief Reconciliation Act of 2001* (P.L. 107-16). In 2008, the maximum permissible catchup contribution to a traditional IRA or Roth IRA is $1,000. The maximum permissible catch-up contribution to a SIMPLE-IRA is $2,500 and the maximum permissible catch-up contribution to a 401(k), 403(b), or 457 plan is $5,000.

Church Plan. A plan established or maintained for its employees by a church or convention of churches exempt from federal tax.

Controlled Group. A controlled group of corporations is any parent-subsidiary or other group of related corporations where 50% or more of such corporations is owned by the same or related persons taking into account only persons with ownership interests of 5% or more.

Current Liability. The *present value of accrued benefits* using an interest assumption that is within a permitted range. There is no consideration of future salary increases or future service.

Defined Benefit Plan. A pension plan that specifies the benefits or the method of determining the benefits, but not the contribution. Specification of benefits can be done in several ways: a specified amount per month for each year of service payable at retirement (dollar benefit); a stated percentage of compensation (fixed benefit); or a stated percentage of compensation for each year of service (unit benefit). Employer contributions to a defined benefit plan are determined actuarially on the basis of the benefits expected to become payable. The company bears the risk of investment performance and must compensate the plan for any shortfalls in funding.

Defined Contribution Plan. A pension plan in which the contributions are specified, but not the benefits. Examples are money purchase plans, *401(k) salary deferral plans*, and profit-sharing plans. Under ERISA, a defined contribution plan (also called "an individual account" plan) is a plan that provides an individual account for each participant that accrues benefits based solely on the amount contributed to the account, and any income, expenses, gains and losses, and reallocation of any forfeitures of accounts of other participants. The employee bears the investment risk.

Early Retirement. Retirement at an age younger than the *normal retirement age* specified in an employee pension benefit plan at which participants may first receive pension benefits. The benefit payable to an early retiree is usually reduced to account for the longer payout period.

Employee Benefit Plan. An employee *welfare* benefit plan or an employee *pension* benefit plan.

Employee Pension Benefit Plan. Any plan, fund, or program established or maintained by an employer or by an employee organization that provides retirement income or that results in the deferral of income.

Employee Stock Ownership Plan (ESOP). An ESOP is a *defined contribution* plan that provides shares of stock in the sponsoring company to participating employees. An ESOP is required to invest primarily in employer stock and is permitted to borrow money on a tax-deductible basis to purchase this stock.

Employee Welfare Benefit Plan. Any plan, fund, or program established or maintained by an employer or by an employee organization that provides through the purchase of insurance or otherwise (a) medical, surgical, or hospital care or benefits in the event of sickness, accident, disability, or death, (b) unemployment or vacation benefits, (c) apprenticeship or other training programs, (d) day care centers, scholarship funds, or prepaid legal services, and (e) "pooled vacation, holiday, severance, or similar benefits" provided by a joint trust fund.

Fiduciary. In the context of ERISA, a fiduciary is a person who exercises any discretionary authority or control with respect to the management of the plan or exercises any authority with respect to the management or disposition of plan assets; (2) renders investment advice for a fee or other compensation with respect to any plan asset or has any authority or responsibility to do so; or (3) has any discretionary responsibility in the administration of the plan.

401(k) Plan. A 401(k) plan, also known as a salary reduction plan or a cash-ordeferred-arrangement (CODA), is a defined contribution plan in which employees may elect to save part of their salaries and defer paying tax on the deferred salary and related investment earnings until the money is taken out of the plan. Companies may make matching or unilateral contributions which are also tax-deferred. Section 401(k) of the tax code was added by the *Revenue Act of 1978* (P.L. 95-600)

403(b) Plan. A 403(b) is a tax deferred retirement annuity available to employees of educational institutions and certain non-profit organizations as determined by Section 501(c)(3) of the Internal Revenue Code. Employee contributions are made on a pre-tax basis and investment earnings grow tax deferred until they are withdrawn, at which time they are taxed as ordinary income. Section 403(b) of the Internal Revenue Code was added by the *Technical Amendments of 1958* (P.L. 85- 866).

457 Plan. A 457 plan is a *nonqualified* deferred compensation plan in which employees of state and local governments or tax-exempt organizations under IRC §501 can defer income on a pre-tax basis. Investment gains accumulate tax-deferred until withdrawn from the plan. A state or local government 457 plan must be made available to all employees, but in many tax-exempt organizations 457 plans are offered to only a select group of employees, in the same manner as a nonqualified plan would be in a private-sector company.

Funding. A systematic program under which assets are set aside in amounts sufficient to assure the future payment of a pension plan's promised benefits.

Governmental Plan. A plan established or maintained by federal, state, or local government, and also any plan to which the *Railroad Retirement Act* applies.

Individual Account Plan. See "Defined Contribution Plan."

Individual Retirement Account (IRA). An IRA can be either an "individual retirement account" or an "individual retirement annuity" There are several types of IRAs: Traditional IRAs, Roth IRAs, SIMPLE IRAs and SEP IRAs. Traditional and Roth IRAs are established by individuals. In 2008, workers can contribute the lesser of $5,000 or 100% of compensation to an IRA. Contributions to a traditional IRA are tax-deductible if the worker's employer does not offer a retirement plan or the worker's family income falls below thresholds set in law. Investment gains accrue on a tax-deferred basis. Withdrawals are taxed as ordinary income and withdrawals before age 59½ may be subject to an additional 10% tax. Contributions to a Roth IRA are not tax-deductible, but distributions from a Roth IRA are tax-free.

Joint and Survivor Annuity. An annuity paid over the joint life expectancy of the participant and spouse. ERISA requires that the annuity payable to the surviving spouse be at least 50% of the reduced annuity paid while the participant was alive. The survivor annuity is automatically provided to a qualifying spouse unless both participant and spouse elect in writing to waive it.

Money Purchase Plan. A type of *defined contribution* plan that provides for fixed contributions. Employer contributions usually are specified a percentage of current compensation and are allocated to individual accounts. The benefits for each employee usually are provided in the form of an annuity based on the amount accumulated in the account including related investment earnings.

Multiemployer Pension Plan. A collectively bargained arrangement in which two or more employers in a particular trade or industry participate in one plan covering a geographical area. These plans are common in the building and construction industry, coal mining, and trucking.

Nonqualified plan. A nonqualified plan is an employer-sponsored retirement plan or deferred compensation plan that does not meet the tax-qualification requirements under Internal Revenue Code §401. A nonqualified plan allows an employee to defer the receipt of income until some future year. For taxes to be deferred, the deferred compensation arrangement must be entered into before the compensation is earned by the employee; the deferred compensation cannot be available to the employee until a previously agreed upon future date or event, and the amount of the deferred compensation cannot be secured and must remain available to the employer's creditors. Nonqualified deferred compensation arrangements are most often established for highly-compensated employees.

Normal Cost. Annual cost of future pension benefits and administrative expenses assigned, under an actuarial cost method, for the year following the plan's valuation date.

Normal Retirement Age. The age, as established by a plan, when retirement occurs with unreduced benefits. Since unreduced Social Security benefits were originally available at age 65, that is the most common *normal retirement age* used in pension plans. ERISA defines "normal retirement age" as the earlier of (a) the age at which a plan participant becomes eligible for retirement under the plan; or (b) the later of (1) the date on which a plan participant attains age 65; or (2) the fifth anniversary of the date on which a plan participant commenced participation.

Party-In-Interest. Includes: (a) any *fiduciary* (administrator, officer, trustee, or custodian), counsel, or employee of an *employee benefit plan*; (b) a person providing services to such plan; (c) an employer, any of whose employees are covered by the plan; (d) a relative of any of the foregoing; and (e) an employee organization, any of whose members are covered by the plan.

Pension Plan Integration. A method for adjusting pension benefits based on the amount a participant receives from Social Security. Social Security benefits are weighted, or tilted, in favor of lower-paid workers. Because the formula of an integrated plan partially reverses the effect of the Social Security tilt, these plans by themselves provide pension benefits in favor of higher-paid workers. A plan generally will meet Internal Revenue Service requirements if the difference in plan benefits between high-paid and low-paid workers is within a "permitted disparity."

PPA. Pension Protection Act of 2006, P.L. 109-280, 120 Stat. 780 (Aug. 17, 2006).

Present Value of Accrued Benefits. The value of benefits accrued to date without consideration of future salary increases or future service, expressed as a lump sum.

Profit-sharing Plan. A profit-sharing plan is a defined contribution plan in which all contributions are made by the employer. Contributions do not have to be related to profits. A company is not obligated to contribute to the plan on a regular basis. Contributions are typically divided among participants in proportion to their earnings, with larger contributions made to higher-paid workers.

Qualified Domestic Relations Order. A judgment, decree, or order (including approval of a property settlement agreement) that (1) relates to the provision of child support, alimony payments, or marital property rights to a spouse, former spouse, child, or other dependent of a participant and (2) is made pursuant to a state domestic relations law (including a community property law).

REA. Retirement Equity Act of 1984, P.L. 98-397, 98 Stat. 1451 (1984). employees.

Safe Harbor 401(k). A safe-harbor 401(k) is exempted from nondiscrimination testing. Employers are required to make fully-vested contributions on behalf of employees. Safe harbor contributions can be structured either as matching contributions or non-elective contributions made on behalf of all plan participants.

SEP IRA. A Simplified Employee Pension, commonly known as a SEP-IRA, is a retirement plan specifically designed for self-employed people and small-business owners. Employer contributions are made into each eligible employee's SEP-IRA. Tax-deductible contributions may total the lesser of 25% of compensation or $46,000 for 2008. All SEP-IRA contributions must be made by the employer, and the same percentage of compensation must be contributed for each eligible employee (based on W-2 wages) including the employer. Annual contributions are not required.

SIMPLE IRA. The SIMPLE IRA is an employer-sponsored retirement plan for businesses with 100 or fewer employees. SIMPLE plans are funded by employer contributions and can be funded by elective employee salary deferrals. Any small business with 100 or fewer employees who earned at least $5,000 in the preceding year can establish a SIMPLE-IRA plan, provided the employer does not concurrently maintain any other employer-sponsored retirement plan. In 2008, eligible employees can elect to contribute the lesser of 100% of compensation or $10,500 through salary reduction. Participants age 50 and older in 2008 may be able to make an additional annual $2,500 contribution to a SIMPLE-IRA. Employers can choose from two different contribution methods. The matching option requires the employer to match each participant's contributions dollar-for-dollar up to 3% of compensation but no more than $10,500 for 2008. The employer can reduce the match to as little as 1% of each participant's compensation for any two years in a five-year period. The non-elective contribution option requires the employer to contribute 2% of each eligible employee's compensation each year, up to a maximum of $4,600 for 2008, regardless of whether the participant contributes or not.

Stock Bonus Plan. A profit-sharing plan that delivers benefits to employees in the form of stock instead of cash.

Target Benefit Plan. A target benefit is a defined contribution plan in which the annual contribution is determined by the amount needed to accumulate (at an assumed rate of interest) sufficient funds to pay a projected retirement benefit — the target benefit — to each participant at retirement age. The contribution to a target benefit plan is based on actuarial assumptions about interest rates, mortality, and employee turnover similar to those used in a defined benefit plan. The contributions to the plan are allocated to separate accounts for each participant. If earnings of the fund differ from those assumed, this does not result in any increase or decrease in employer contributions; instead, it increases or decreases the benefits payable to the participant. An employee's age is one of the factors that determines the size of the contributions. Employer contributions to a target benefit plan are larger for older employees than for younger employees.

Thrift Plan (or Savings Plan). A thrift plan is an employee-funded savings plan. An employee generally makes contributions, often stated as a percentage of pay, to an account established in his or her name. The contributions may be matched in full or in part by the employer, but there is no legal requirement for employer contributions. Prior to the *Revenue Act of 1978*, employee contributions to thrift plans were made on an after-tax basis. The 1978 law added Section 401(k) to the Internal Revenue Code, which allowed income taxes to be deferred on employee contributions to these plans.

Vesting. Earning a nonforfeitable right to a pension benefit. A plan must provide that an employee will retain, after meeting certain requirements, a right to at least some, and perhaps all, of the benefits he/she has accrued, even if the employee ceases employment under the plan before reaching the eligibility age for benefits. An employee who has met such requirements is said to have a "vested" or "nonforfeitable" right to benefits. Voluntary and mandatory employee contributions are always fully vested when received by the plan.

End Notes

[1] P.L. 93-406, 88 Stat. 829 (Sept. 2, 1974). ERISA is codified at §§1001 to 1453 of title 29, United States Code and in § § 401-415 and 4972-4975 of the Internal Revenue Code.

[2] See ERISA § 3(1), (29 U.S.C. § 1002), for the different types of welfare benefit plans.

[3] When a plan participant receives income from a pension plan, it is taxable income.

[4] Federal law limits the extent to which pension benefits can be reduced as a result of "integration" of the benefits with Social Security benefits. See 26 U.S.C. § 401(l).

[5] *Inland Steel Co. v. National Labor Relations Board*, 170 F.2d 247 (7th Cir. 1948). *cert. denied*, 336 U.S. 960 (1949).

[6] P.L. 85-836, 72 Stat. 997 (Aug. 29, 1958).

[7] 29 U.S.C. § 1002(34) and § 1002(35); 26 U.S.C. § 414(i) and § 414(j).

[8] 26 U.S.C. § 4 14(i).

[9] P.L. 95-600, 92 Stat. 2826 (Nov. 6, 1978).

[10] See "Benefit Accrual and Age Discrimination" in section III for additional discussion of hybrid plans.

[11] IRC §401(k) authorizes "cash or deferred arrangements," under which an employee may elect to have the employer make payments as contributions to a trust fund on behalf of the employee in lieu of receiving that portion of his or her compensation in cash.

[12] Salary deferral plans under IRC §403(b) and §457 predate §401(k), but these plans are available only to employees of tax-exempt organizations and state and local governments.

[13] An exception to this rule is the "money purchase plan," which is a DC plan but also is a pension plan established under IRC §401(a), and must offer plan participants an annuity.

[14] Some firms automatically enroll all eligible employees in their 401(k) plans, so that the default condition is for the employee to be enrolled with the option to quit the plan.

[15] For more information, see CRS Report RL33703, *Summary of the Pension Protection Act of 2006*, by Patrick Purcell.

[16] ERISA § 4, 29 U.S.C. § 1003.

[17] *See* ERISA § 101*et. seq*., 29 U.S.C. § 1021 *et. seq*. and accompanying regulations. Certain types of employee benefit plans are exempt or partially exempt from the main reporting and disclosure requirements of ERISA. These plans include unfunded or insured welfare plans that provide benefits for a select group of management or highly compensated employees, as well as plans that exclusively provide apprenticeship training benefits or other training benefits. *See* 29 C.F.R. § 2520.104.

It should also be noted that additional reporting and disclosure provisions exist under other sections of ERISA. *See, e.g.,* COBRA, P.L. 99-272, 100 Stat. 82 (1986), which requires health plans to issue notices related to continued medical insurance coverage. ERISA § 606, 29 U.S.C. § 1166.

[18] P.L. 109-280, 120 Stat. 780 (Aug. 17, 2006).
[19] 29 U.S.C. § 1025(a)(1).
[20] ERISA § 101, 29 U.S.C. § 1021; 124 A.L.R. Fed. 355 (*citing Hicks v Fleming Cos.*, 961 F.2d 537 (5th Cir. 1992)).
[21] 124 A.L.R. Fed. 355.
[22] ERISA § 102(a)(1), 29 USC 1022(a)(1); *See also* S.Rept. 93-127, 2d Sess, (Apr. 18, 1973).
[23] *Hicks v. Fleming Cos.*, 961 F.2d 537 (5th Cir. 1992).
[24] 29 U.S.C. § 1024(b)(1), ERISA § 102(a); 29 U.S.C. § 1022(a); 29 C.F.R. § 2520.104b-3.
[25] ERISA § 104(b)(1), 29 U.S.C. § 1024(b)(1); 29 C.F.R. § 2520.104a-8.
[26] However, regulations provide a special rule for health plans. Subject to an exception, an SMM shall be furnished if there is a "material reduction in covered services or benefits." 29 C.F.R. § 2520.104b-3.
[27] EMPLOYEE BENEFITS LAW (Matthew Bender 2d ed.)(2000).
[28] *See, e.g., Baker v. Lukens Steel Co.*, 793 F.2d 509 (3rd Cir. 1986)(elimination of an early retirement benefit option was a material modification); *American Fed 'n of Grain Millers v. International Multifoods Corp.*, 1996 U.S. Dist. LEXIS 9399 (W.D.N.Y. 1996) *aff'd*, 116 F.3d 976 (2d Cir. 1997) (amendment to a medical plan requiring retirees to pay a portion of premiums considered a material modification).
[29] *See, e.g., Hasty v. Central States, Southeast and Southwest Areas Health and Welfare Fund*, 851 F. Supp. 1250, 1256 (N.D. Ind. 1994) (amendments more specifically providing for a trustee's discretionary authority under an employee benefit plan were not a material modification because the amendments "simply clarify a power").
[30] ERISA § 103; 29 U.S.C. § 1023. Labor Department regulations exempt some plans from the annual reporting requirement. For example, welfare benefit plans having fewer than 100 participants may be exempted if certain conditions are met. 29 C.F.R. § 2520.104-20.
[31] 72 Fed. Reg. 64710 (Nov. 16, 2007).
[32] *Id.*
[33] ERISA § 104(b), 29 U.S.C.§ 1024(b).
[34] ERISA § 104(b)(2), 29 U.S.C.§ 1024(b)(2). Under this section, other materials, such as a bargaining agreement or trust agreement affecting the plan may also be made available.
[35] See 29 C.F.R. § 2520.104a-5.
[36] While ERISA and the Internal Revenue Code provide that other annual reports must be filed with the PBGC and the Internal Revenue Service, these reporting requirements can be satisfied by filing Form 5500 with the Labor Department.
[37] 29 C.F.R. § 2520.104a-2.
[38] ERISA provides an exception to this requirement for one-participant retirement plans. ERISA § 105; 29 U.S.C. § 1025.
[39] Under this section, beneficiaries of a plan that do not fall into either category can request a pension benefit statement from a plan administrator. ERISA § 105, 29 U.S.C. § 1025.
[40] ERISA§ 101(f), 29 U.S.C. § 1021(f).
[41] Information required to be on a plan's funding notice is different, depending on whether the plan in question is a single-employer or multi-employer plan. *See* ERISA § 101 (f)(2)(B), 29 U.S.C. § 1021(f)(2)(B).
[42] 29 U.S.C. § 1021(m).
[43] Section 410 of the Internal Revenue Code contains similar participation requirements. See 26 U.S.C. § 410(a). Section 410 also contains coverage rules intended to ensure that a pension plan covers both highly compensated employees and other employees proportionately. 26 U.S.C. § 410(b). Participation and coverage requirements must be met in order for a plan to be considered qualified (*i.e.*, eligible for favorable tax treatment).
[44] Courts have found that ERISA's minimum participation requirements only prevent employers from denying participation in a plan on basis of age or length of service. These requirements do not prevent employers from denying plan participation on any other basis. As stated by the Third Circuit in *Bauer v. Summit Bancorp*, "In fact, an employer could even exclude all

persons whose names begin with the letter 'H,' as long as this was not deemed to be discriminatory in application." 325 F.3d 155, 166 n.2 (3rd Cir. 2003).

[45] An employee's eligibility to participate in a pension plan may be affected if there is a break in the employee's period of service. ERISA 202(b), 29 U.S.C. § 1052(b). For example, if an employee has had a one-year break in service, a plan is not required to take into account any previous service performed in calculating the employee's period of service. A one-year break in service is a 12-consecutive-month period in which the employee has not completed more than 500 hours of service. ERISA § 203(b)(3)(A), 29 U.S.C. § 1053(b)(3)(A).

[46] For information on the vesting of benefits under ERISA, see discussion under "Minimum Vesting Standards" in section IV *infra.*

[47] This variation is not available for 40 1(k) plans. Under §401(k)(2)(D), an employee with one year of service must be allowed to elect to make pre-tax contributions to the plan.

[48] ERISA § 202(a)(1)(B)(ii), 29 U.S.C. § 1052(a)(1)(B)(ii).

[49] ERISA § 202(a)(4), 29 U.S.C. § 1052(a)(4).

[50] ERISA § 202(a)(2), 29 U.S.C. § 1052(a)(2).

[51] In *DiGiacomo v. Teamsters Pension Trust Fund*, 420 F.3d 220, 223 (3rd Cir. 2005), Justice Alito, in his former position as a Third Circuit Judge, stated that accrued benefits, "are like chalk marks beside the employee's name ... they are conditional rights that do not become irrevocabl[e] ... until they vest."

[52] ERISA § 3(23)(A), 29 U.S.C. § 1002(23)(A).

[53] ERISA § 204(b)(1), 29 U.S.C. § 1054(b)(1), 26 U.S.C. § 411(b). *See also* 26 C.F.R. § 1.411(b)-1.

[54] *See* ERISA § 3(23), 29 U.S.C. § 1002(23)(B).

[55] See section I(C) discussing ERISA's participation requirements.

[56] See ERISA § 204(c), 29 U.S.C. § 1054(c).

[57] 29 U.S.C. § 1054(g).

[58] Certain exceptions to the anti-cutback rule may apply. For example, ERISA allows for a plan to reduce accrued benefits by a retroactive amendment in certain cases where a plan is confronted with a "substantial business hardship." ERISA § 204(g)(1), 29 U.S.C. § 1054(g)(1) (*citing* ERISA § 302(d)(2), 29 U.S.C. § 1082(d)(2)).

[59] Patrick C. DiCarlo, ERISA'S ANTI-CUTBACK RULE: THE PITFALLS OF PLAN MODIFICATION, 60 Employee Benefit Plan Review 5 (2006).

[60] *Central Laborers' Pension Fund v. Heinz*, 541 U.S. 739 (2004).

[61] *Id.* at 745.

[62] Age discrimination provisions are also included in the Internal Revenue Code and the Age Discrimination in Employment Act. *See* IRC § 41 1(b)(1)(H); 29 U.S.C. § 623(i)(1). Although the language under all three laws is not identical, these laws are intended to be interpreted in the same manner. H. Rep. 99-727 at 378-79; P.L. 99-509, § 9204(d).

[63] A cash balance plan is a "hybrid plan," (*i.e.*, a plan that has characteristics of both defined benefit and defined contribution plans). Cash balance plans are defined benefit plans that look like defined contribution plans because the employee's accrued benefit is stated as an account balance. In a cash balance plan, the "account balance" is a record of the benefit accrued by the participant, but it is not an individual account owned by the participant.

[64] *IBM Pers. Pension Plan v. Cooper*, 457 F.3d 636 (7th Cir. 2006), *rev 'ing* 274 F. Supp. 2d 1010 (S.D. Ill. 2003), *cert. denied*, 2007 U.S. LEXIS 1140 (U.S. Jan. 16, 2007); *Register v. PNC Fin. Servs. Group, Inc.*, 477 F.3d 56 (3rd Cir. 2007); *Drutis v. Rand McNally & Co.*, 499 F.3d 608, 610 (6th Cir. 2007), *but see*, *In re J.P. Morgan Chase Cash Balance Litig.*, 460 F. Supp. 2d 479, 482 (D.N.Y. 2006).

[65] ERISA § 204(b)(5), 29 U.S.C. § 1054(c); IRC § 411(b)(5); 29 U.S.C. § 623(i)(10).

[66] For more information on this issue, see CRS Report RL33004, *Cash Balance Plans and Claims of Age Discrimination*, by Erika Lunder and Jennifer Staman.

[67] There can be confusion in understanding the difference between when benefits accrue and when benefits vest. As articulated by the Supreme Court, accrual is "the rate at which an

employee earns benefits to put in his pension account." *Central Laborers' Pension Fund v. Heinz*, 541 U.S. 739, 749 (2004). Vesting, on the other hand, is "the process by which an employee's already-accrued pension account becomes irrevocably his property." *Id.*

[68] Parallel vesting provisions may be found in Internal Revenue Code § 411.

[69] "Normal retirement benefit", as defined by Section 3(22) of ERISA, means the greater of an early retirement benefit offered under the plan or the benefit under the plan commencing at normal retirement age.

[70] While normal retirement age under a plan can be a specific age, it also may include service requirements (*e.g.*, 55 years old with at least five years of service). *See also* 26 U.S.C. § 411(a)(8).

[71] ERISA § 3(24), 29 U.S.C. § 1002(24). It should also be noted that the Treasury Department has recently issued regulations regarding distributions from a qualified pension plan upon attainment of normal retirement age. *See* 72 Fed. Reg. 28604 (May 22, 2007), 26 C.F.R. § 1.401(a)-1(b).

[72] 29 U.S.C. § 1053.

[73] ERISA § 203(a)(2)(A); 29 U.S.C. § 1053(a)(2)(A). *See* ERISA § 203(b); 29 U.S.C. § 1053(b), for requirements relating to computing a participant's period of service. This section provides that in computing the period of service for purposes of the vesting requirement, all years of service must be taken into account, subject to certain exceptions and limitations.

[74] A year of service means a consecutive 12 month period during which a participant has completed 1,000 hours of service.

[75] ERISA § 203(a)(2)(B), 29 U.S.C. § 1053(a)(2)(B).

[76] *See* 26 U.S.C. § 401(m)(4).

[77] ERISA § 203(b), 29 U.S.C. § 1053(b).

[78] ERISA § 203(b)(3)(E), 29 U.S.C. § 1053(b)(3)(E).

[79] P.L. 98-397, 98 Stat. 1451 (1984).

[80] ERISA § 205, 29 U.S.C. § 1055, and 26 U.S.C. § 417. Payment to a married participant in a DB plan of a single-life annuity or a lump sum requires the spouse's written consent.

[81] ERISA § 206, 29 U.S.C. § 1056. ERISA § 206(d) also provides that with the exception of a QDRO, benefits provided by a pension plan may not be assigned or garnished.

[82] ERISA § 205(d), 29 U.S.C. § 1055(d), as amended by Section 1004 of the PPA.

[83] ERISA § 206, 29 U.S.C. § 1056, as amended by § 104 of the REA of 1984.

[84] §1001 of the PPA.

[85] ERISA § 208, 29 U.S.C. § 1058.

[86] ERISA §§302 through 308 govern funding of defined benefit pension plans. (Also see 26 U.S.C. § 412, §430, §431, and §432.) Funding requirements for single-employer plans were amended by § § 101 to 116 of the PPA. Funding requirements for multiemployer DB plans were amended by §§201 to 221 of the PPA.

[87] Deficit reduction contributions (DRCs) were additional contributions required of underfunded plans prior to enactment of the PPA. The PPA eliminated DRCs after 2007.

[88] ERISA § 303, 29 U.S.C. § 1083, as amended by §102 of the PPA.

[89] A yield curve is a graph that shows interest rates on bonds plotted against the maturity date of the bond. Normally, long-term bonds have higher yields than short-term bonds because both credit risk and inflation risk rise as the maturity dates extend further into the future. Consequently, the yield curve usually slopes upward from left to right.

[90] P.L. 108-218, 118 Stat. 596 (Apr. 10, 2004).

[91] The PPA extended the interest rates permissible under P.L. 108-218 through 2007 for purposes of the current liability calculation.

[92] ERISA § 303, 29 U.S.C. § 1083, as amended by §102 of the PPA.

[93] ERISA § 303, 29 U.S.C. § 1083 as amended by §102 of the PPA.

[94] A credit balance in a plan at the end of the 2007 plan year is referred to as a "carryover balance." A credit balance created after 2007 is referred to as a "prefunding balance."

[95] ERISA § 206, 29 U.S.C. § 1056 as amended by §103 of the PPA.

[96] In 2004, the 6th Circuit Court of Appeals ruled that the PBGC could set a plan termination date that would prevent the agency from being liable for shutdown benefits. *PBGC v. Republic Technologies International, LLC, et al.*, 386 F.3d 659 (6th Cir. 2004). In March 2005, the Supreme Court declined to hear the case, leaving the Circuit Court's decision in place.

[97] ERISA § 205(g), 26 U.S.C. § 4 17(e), as amended by § 302 of the PPA.

[98] IRC §415 sets limitations on benefits and contributions in qualified plans.

[99] For more detailed information of the effect of the PPA on lump-sums, see CRS Report RS22765, *Lump-sum Distributions under the Pension Protection Act*, by Patrick Purcell.

[100] Funding requirements for multiemployer plans were amended by §§201-221 of the PPA.

[101] *See* 29 C.F.R. § 2510.3-21, which provides guidance as to when a person shall be deemed to be rendering investment advice to an employee benefit plan.

[102] Plan fiduciaries may include plan trustees, plan administrators, and a plan's investment managers or advisors. *See* Department of Labor, Fiduciary Responsibilities, *available at* [https://www.dol.gov/dol/topic/retirement

[103] ERISA § 402(a), 29 U.S.C. § 1102(a).

[104] ERISA § 404(a)(1), 29 U.S.C. § 1 104(a)(1).

[105] This section is supplemented by Section 403(c)(1) of ERISA, which provides that the "assets of a plan shall never inure to the benefit of any employer and shall be held for the exclusive purposes of providing benefits ... and defraying reasonable expenses of administering the plan." 29 U.S.C. § 1103(c)(1).

[106] Craig C. Martin & Elizabeth L. Fine, *ERISA Stock Drop Cases: An Evolving Standard,* 38 J. Marshall L. Rev. 889 (2005).

[107] *Id.*

[108] 680 F.2d 263 (2nd Cir. 1982).

[109] 680 F.2d at 271.

[110] *Id.*

[111] ERISA § 404(a)(1)(A)(ii), 29 U.S.C. § 1 104(a)(1)(A)(ii).

[112] U.S. Department of Labor, Employee Benefits Security Administration, Information Letter, July 28, 1998. [http://www.dol.gov/ebsa/regs/ILs/il072898.html].

[113] 72 Fed. Reg. 64731 (Nov. 16, 2007).

[114] 72 Fed. Reg. 70988 (Dec. 13, 2007).

[115] 29 U.S.C. § 1 104(a)(1)(B).

[116] *See, e.g., GIW Industries v. Trevor, Stewart, Burton & Jacobsen*, 895 F.2d 729 (11th Cir. 1990) (investment management firm breached its duty of prudence after investing primarily in long-term, low risk government bonds and failing to take into account the liquidity needs of the plan); *Donovan v. Mazzola*, 716 F.2d 1226, 1232 (9th Cir. 1983) (court stated that test of prudence is whether "at the time they engaged in the challenged transactions, [fiduciaries] employed the appropriate methods to investigate the merits of the investment and to structure the investment").

[117] *See, e.g., Unisys,* 74 F.3d at 434 ("[I]f at the time an investment is made, it is an investment a prudent person would make, there is no liability if the investment later depreciates in value").

[118] *See* 29 C.F.R. § 2550.404a-1.

[119] *Id.*

[120] 29 U.S.C. § 1 104(a)(1)(C).

[121] *See generally*, H.R. Rep. No. 1280 at 304 (1974), *reprinted in* 1974 U.S.C.C.A.N. 5085.

[122] 155 A.L.R. Fed. 349 (2007).

[123] 895 F.2d 729 (11th Cir. 1990).

[124] *GIW Industries*, 895 F.2d at 733.

[125] 841 F.2d 344 (10th Cir. 1988).

[126] *Metzler v. Graham*, 112 F.3d 207 (5th Cir. 1997).

[127] The court in *Graham* maintained that the trustee's investment was prudent under the circumstances and thus, within the exception in Section 404(a)(1)(C). The court identified

four factors that supported the position that Graham did not "imprudently introduce a risk of large loss by purchasing the Property."*Graham*, 112 F.3d at 210. First, there was no requirement that the plan make payments to beneficiaries until age 65, death, or disability, and the average age of the plan participants was 37 when the property was purchased. Remaining plan assets were available to cover projected payouts for the next twenty years. Second, the purchase was better insulated from the possible return of high inflation: "when the plan's holdings consisted solely of cash and short term instruments, there was little hedge against inflation." *Id.* at 211. Third, there was a significant cushion between the purchase price and the property's appraised value. Finally, the trustee's expertise in the development of industrial property supported the conclusion that the investment was prudent. After considering these fact\ors, the court was persuaded that the investment did not carry a risk of large loss.

[128] 29 U.S.C. § 1 104(a)(1)(D).

[129] *See* Employee Benefits Guide, Matthew Bender & Company, Inc. §24.15 (2007).

[130] See George A. Norwood, *Who Is Entitled to Receive a Deceased Participant's ERISA Retirement Plan Benefits - an Ex-Spouse or Current Spouse? The Federal Circuits Have an Irreconcilable Conflict*, 33 Gonz. L. Rev. 61, 75 (1997-1998).

[131] *See, e.g., Cent. States v. Cent. Transp*., 472 U.S. 559, 569 (1985)(stating that "trust documents cannot excuse trustees from their duties under ERISA, and ... trust documents must generally be construed in light of ERISA's policies. [S]ee 29 U. S. C. § 1 104(a)(1)(D)...").

[132] Department of Labor Brief for Amicus, Nos. 04-1082, 03-155331 (4th Cir. 2004).

[133] 284 F. Supp. 2d 511, 2003 U.S. Dist. LEXIS 17492, 31 Employee Benefits Cas. (BNA) 2281 (S.D. Tex. 2003).

[134] *Enron* at 669-70 (as cited in Department of Labor Brief for Amicus, Nos. 04-1082, 03-15533 1 (4th Cir. 2004)).

[135] 975 F.2d 1467(10th Cir. 1992).

[136] *Harris Trust and Sav. Bank v. Salomon Smith Barney, Inc*., 530 U.S. 238 (2000). The Internal Revenue Code also contains certain prohibited transaction provisions. *See* 26 U.S.C. § 4975.

[137] *See, e.g., Cutaiar v. Marshall*, 590 F.2d 523 (3d Cir. 1979).

[138] ERISA defines "party in interest" quite broadly to include a number of individuals who could affect a plan or its fiduciaries. *See* ERISA § 3(14), 29 U.S.C. § 1002(14).

[139] Exceptions to the prohibited transactions provisions may be found in Section 408 of ERISA (29 U.S.C. § 1108).

[140] 29 U.S.C. § 1106(b).

[141] "Qualifying employer security," as defined in Section 407(d)(5) (29 U.S.C. § 11 07(d)(5)) means an employer security which is (A) stock, (B) a marketable obligation (*i.e.,* a bond, debenture, note, or certificate, or other evidence of indebtedness, subject to certain acquisition requirements described in 407(e)), or (C) an interest in a publicly traded partnership (as defined in Section 7704(b) of the Internal Revenue Code) if it is an "existing partnership." *See* 26 U.S.C. § 7704 note. Qualifying employer securities may have to meet additional requirements. *See* ERISA § 407(d)(5)(C).

[142] Property may be deemed "qualifying employer real property" under Section 407(d)(4) of ERISA (29 U.S.C. § 1 107(d)(4)) if a substantial number of the parcels are dispersed geographically; each parcel of real property and the improvements thereon are suitable (or adaptable without excessive cost) for more than one use; without regard to whether all of such real property is leased to one lessee; and if the acquisition and retention of such property comply with the provisions of ERISA (subject to certain exceptions).

[143] *See* ERISA § 407(b)(1), 29 U.S.C. 407(b)(1), which is applicable to plans that require a portion of an elective deferral to be used to acquire qualifying employer securities, qualifying real property, or both.

[144] 29 U.S.C. § 1054(j). The requirements of this section may not apply to certain defined contribution plans, including certain ESOPs and one-participant plans (as defined in ERISA § 101(i)(8)(B), 29 U.S.C. § 1021(i)(8)(B)).

[145] Thus, employer contributions acquired in a plan year before January 1, 2007, may be divested as follows: 33% in the first plan year, 66% in the second year, and 100% in the third and following plan year. Participants who reached age 55 before the 2006 plan year are exempt from the phasing requirement.

[146] ERISA, as originally enacted, provided for both the Department of Labor and Department of Treasury to issue prohibited transactions exemptions. This was limited in 1979 by Reorganization Plan No. 4 of 1978 102(a), 43 Fed. Reg. 47,713 (1978). Under this Reorganization Plan, the Treasury Department transferred almost all of its interpretive and exemptive authority over the Internal Revenue Code's prohibited transaction rules to the Department of Labor. Currently, the Labor Department evaluates virtually all of the applications for administrative exemptions.

[147] *See* 29 C.F.R. § 2570.30 *et. seq.*

[148] ERISA § 408(b)(1), 29 U.S.C. § 1108.

[149] *See* H.Rept. 107-262 pt. 1, at 12-13 (2001).

[150] *Id.* at 12 (2001).

[151] *See* ERISA § 408(g)(3)(B), 29 U.S.C. §1108(g)(3)(B). For additional information on Investment Advice under the PPA, see CRS Report RS22514, *Investment Advice and the Pension Protection Act of 2006*, by Jon O. Shimabukuro.

[152] Under Section 404(c), plan fiduciaries are only shielded from liability for losses "which result from" a participant or beneficiary's investment choices. A 404(c) plan fiduciary still remains liable for other fiduciary obligations. For example, a plan fiduciary still must select appropriate investment alternatives from which plan participants may choose, and monitor the performance of these investments. The Department of Labor, in promulgating regulations for ERISA §404(c), emphasized this point:

... the act of designating investment alternatives ... in an ERISA Section 404(c) plan is a fiduciary function to which the limitation on liability provided by Section 404(c) is not applicable. All of the fiduciary provisions of ERISA remain applicable to both the initial designation of investment alternatives and investment managers and the ongoing determination that such alternatives and managers remain suitable and prudent investment alternatives for the plan. Therefore, the particular plan fiduciaries responsible for performing these functions must do so in accordance with ERISA. 57 Fed. Reg. 46906 (Oct. 13, 1992).

[153] 29 C.F.R. § 2550.404c-1. This section is hereinafter referred to as "the 404(c) regulations."

[154] 29 C.F.R. § 2550.404c-1(b)(i).

[155] 29 C.F.R. § 2550.404c-1(b)(2)(B).

[156] 29 C.F.R. § 2550.404c-1(b)(ii).

[157] *Id.*

[158] 29 C.F.R. § 2550.404c-1(b)(3). Because employer stock is not a diversified investment, it cannot be one of the three "core" investment options required by ERISA Section 404(c). *See* section I(I) *supra* for discussion of diversification requirements on certain defined contribution plans that hold employer securities.

[159] 29 C.F.R. § 2550.404c-1(c)(1). The 404(c) regulations specify that a participant or beneficiary will be deemed to have exercised control with respect to the exercise of voting, tender, and other rights related to an investment, provided that the participant or beneficiary had a reasonable opportunity to exercise control in making the investment.

[160] 29 C.F.R. § 2550.404c-1(c)(2). Circumstances under which a participant or beneficiary's control will not be considered independent include situations where the individual is subject to improper influence by a plan fiduciary or plan sponsor with respect to a transaction, or where a plan fiduciary has concealed "material non-public facts" regarding the investment, unless such disclosure would violate federal or state law.

[161] ERISA § 409, 29 U.S.C. § 1109. For a discussion of actions that may be brought under ERISA in the event of fiduciary breach, see the "Administration and Enforcement" section *infra*.

[162] 29 U.S.C. § 1109. Section 409 works in conjunction with Section 502 of ERISA, ERISA's primary civil enforcement provision. See *supra* section I(I) on "Fiduciary Duty." Section 502(a)(2) allows for a civil action to be brought "by the Secretary, or by a participant, beneficiary, or fiduciary for appropriate relief under § 409."

[163] EMPLOYEE BENEFITS LAW (Matthew Bender 2d ed.)(2000). (*citing Aull v. Cavalcade*, 988 F. Supp. 1360 (D. Colo. 1997); *Davidson v. Cook*, 567 F. Supp. 225 (E.D. Va. 1983), *aff'd*, 734 F.2d 10, (4th Cir. 1984), *cert. denied*, 469 U.S. 899 (1984)).

[164] See, e.g., *Morrison v. Curran*, 567 F. 2d 546 (2nd Cir. 1977)(court evaluated an improper use of plan assets made prior to ERISA; court opined that "trustee's obligation to dispose of improper investments within a reasonable time is well established at common law" and that " ERISA can hardly be read to eviscerate this duty"). *See also McDougall v. Donovan*, 552 F. Supp. 1206, 1212 (D. Ill. 1982). *But see Beauchem v. Rockford Prods. Corp.*, 2004 U.S. Dist. LEXIS 2091 (D. Ill. 2004)(In dismissing a claim against defendant co-fiduciaries, court stated that "[a]llowing a fiduciary to be liable for failing to correct a breach committed by prior fiduciaries would destroy the protection of section [409](b)").
While not addressed in this chapter, a fiduciary may also be responsible for an act of a co-fiduciary under Section 405 of ERISA. This section contains various circumstances under which a fiduciary can be liable for a breach of responsibility made by another fiduciary. 29 U.S.C. § 1105.

[165] See ERISA § 2, 29 U.S.C. § 1001.

[166] ERISA § 2(b), 29 U.S.C. § 1001(b). *See also Aetna Health Inc. v. Davila*, 542 U.S. 200, 208 (2004).

[167] *Russell*, 473 U.S., at 147.

[168] *Aetna Health Inc. v. Davila*, 542 U.S. at 208.

[169] 29 U.S.C. § 1132. ERISA's enforcement scheme extends beyond civil actions. Other methods of enforcement include tax disqualification and criminal sanctions.

[170] *See* Section 502(a) (29 U.S.C. 1132(a)) for additional civil actions authorized by ERISA. *See* 502(c)(29 U.S.C. § 1132(c)) for circumstances under which the Secretary of Labor may assess a civil penalty.

[171] *Metropolitan Life Insurance Co. v. Taylor*, 481 U.S. 58, 63-4 (1987).

[172] *Gaming Corp. of Am. v. Dorsey & Whitney*, 88 F.3d 536, 543 (8th Cir. 1996) (*citing Taylor*, 481 U.S. 58 at 65; *Avco Corp. v. Aero Lodge No. 735, Intern. Ass 'n of Machinists and Aerospace Workers*, 390 U.S. 557 (1968).

[173] The procedure for determining whether a case will be moved from state court to federal court is governed by Section 1441(a) of the Federal Rules of Civil Procedure (FRCP). Under FRCP § 144 1(a), any civil action brought in state court may be removed to federal district court if the defendants can show that the federal district court has original jurisdiction. 28 U.S.C. § 144 1(a). Courts follow the "well-pleaded complaint rule," which allows the plaintiff to determine whether an action is heard in state or federal court. The plaintiff is able to choose his forum because "[i]t is long settled law that a cause of action arises under federal law only when the plaintiff's well-pleaded complaint raises issues of federal law." *Taylor*, 481 U.S. at 63. The fact that the defendant's defense arises under federal law is not enough to move the case to federal court. However, under the doctrine of complete preemption, a state claim may be removed to federal court if Congress has completely preempted a particular area.

[174] See section I(K) of this chapter for a broader discussion of preemption, including discussion of Section 514 of ERISA, ERISA's express preemption provision.

[175] Jayne E. Zanglein, Susan J. Stabile, 31 JOURNAL OF PENSION PLANNING AND COMPLIANCE 1 (2005).

[176] *Pilot Life Ins. Co. v. Dedeaux*, 481 U.S. 41, 43 (1987).

[177] See section I(L) for a discussion of ERISA § 514, ERISA's express preemption provision.
[178] *Pilot Life*, 481 U.S. at 54.
[179] *Aetna Health Inc. v. Davila*, 542 U.S. 200 (2004).
[180] *Id.*
[181] *Id.*
[182] ERISA § 409, 29 U.S.C. § 1109.
[183] *Mass. Mut. Life Ins. Co. v. Russell*, 473 U.S. 134, 140 (1985).
[184] *Id.*
[185] In its decision the Court noted that it declined to decide "the extent to which section 409 may authorize recovery of extracontractual compensatory or punitive damages from a fiduciary by a *plan*. 473 U.S. 134, 144 n. 12 (1985). *See also Mertens v. Hewitt Assocs*., 508 U.S. 248 (1993) (in a dissenting opinion, Justice White observed that courts are split on whether punitive damages may be recovered under ERISA 502(a)(2)). *Mertens*, 508 U.S. at 273 n.6 (White, J., dissenting)).
[186] *LaRue v. DeWolff, Boberg & Associates*, 2008 LEXIS 2014 (2008).
[187] *Id.* at 9 (*quoting Russell*, 473 U.S. at 142).
[188] In addition, as the Court points out, unlike *LaRue,* the plaintiff in *Russell* received all the benefits to which she was entitled.
[189] While the plan at issue in *Russell* was a disability plan rather than a defined benefit plan, the Court applied the logic in *Russell* to defined benefit plans. *See id*. at 12-13.
[190] *Id.* at 12.
[191] *Id*. Although all of the Justices agreed on the outcome of the *LaRue* case, they disagreed as to the reasoning behind it. See *LaRue* 2008 U.S. LEXIS 2014, 17 (2008) (Roberts, J. concurring) and 2008 U.S. LEXIS 2014, 20 (Thomas, J. concurring). For additional discussion of this case, see CRS Report RS22827, *Liability of Plan Fiduciaries under ERISA : LaRue v. DeWolff, Boberg & Associates*, by Jennifer Staman.
[192] Courts sometimes determine whether the relief a plaintiff seeks is legal or equitable. Colleen Murphy, *Money as a "Specific" Remedy*, 58 Ala. L. Rev. 119, 134 (2006). This distinction dates back to the "days of the divided bench," when England (and subsequently the United States) maintained separate courts of law and courts of equity. *See generally Great-West Life & Annuity Ins. Co. v. Knudson*, 534 U.S. 204, 212 (2002). One important way these courts differed from each other was the remedies available to plaintiffs. Historically, the most common remedy in the courts of law was money. *Id.* at 135. The most common remedy in the courts of equity was an order for an individual to do something or refrain from doing something, such as with an injunction. *Id*. The scope of remedies available at law and at equity have been the subject of debate. While there is no longer this divided court system, courts may still evaluate a claim based on this dichotomy.
[193] *See Varity Corp. v. Howe*, 516 U.S. 489 (1996).
[194] *Id.*
[195] Roy F. Harmon III, 'Equitable Relief' Claims under ERISA Section 502(a)(3), 20 Benefits Law Journal 33 (2007).
[196] 508 U.S. 248 (1993).
[197] *See id*. at 255, 256.
[198] *Great-West Life & Annuity Ins. Co. v. Knudson*, 534 U.S. 204 (2002).
[199] This type of claim is referred to as a subrogation claim. For additional discussion of a subrogation claim, *see* footnote 231 *infra* and accompanying text.
[200] "Restitution" has been defined as "return or restoration of some specific thing to its rightful owner or status." Black's Law Dictionary 1315 (7th ed. 1999). It has been noted that restitution is an ambiguous term, sometimes referring to the disgorging of something which has been taken and at times referring to compensation for injury done." *Id.* (*citing* John D. Calamari and Joseph M. Perillo, THE LAW OF CONTRACTS, § 9-23 at 376 (3d. Ed. 1987).

[201] *Cf. Sereboff v. Mid-Atlantic Services*, 547 U.S. 356 (2006) in which the Supreme Court found health plan administrators were entitled to equitable relief under Section 502(a)(3). Similar to the *Great West* case, in *Sereboff*, plan participants were in an automobile accident, and their health plan paid medical expenses on the participant's behalf. Later, after the participants had received a settlement amount arising from a claim brought because of the accident, the health plan sought reimbursement from plan participants. In finding that the relief sought by the administrators was equitable under Section 502(a)(3), the Court distinguished the *Sereboff* case from *Great West* because, among other things, the amounts in question in Sereboff were identifiable, as they were set aside in an investment account.

[202] 29 U.S.C. § 1021 *et seq.*

[203] 29 U.S.C. § 1131.

[204] EMPLOYEE BENEFITS LAW 1400 (Matthew Bender 2d ed.)(2000).

[205] 29 U.S.C. § 1141.

[206] Crimes that prevent an individual from service with an employee benefit plan include robbery, bribery, embezzlement, murder, perjury, crimes that disqualify individuals from serving as an investment advisor (see 15 U.S.C. § 80a-9(a)(1)), as well as violations of ERISA. *See* 29 U.S.C. § 1111(a).

[207] *Id.*

[208] *Id.*

[209] 18 U.S.C. § 1954.

[210] 29 U.S.C. § 1136(b).

[211] ERISA § 506(a), 29 U.S.C. § 1136(a).

[212] *Travelers,* 514 U.S. at 657.

[213] *See Alessi v. Raybestos-Manhattan*, Inc., 451 U.S. 504, 523 (1981), as cited in *New York State Conf. of Blue Cross & Blue Shield Plans v. Travelers Ins.* Co., 514 U.S. 645, 656 (1995).

[214] ERISA and Health Plans, Employee Benefits Research Institute, *available at* [http://www.ebri.org/pdf/briefspdf/1195ib.pdf].

[215] 463 U.S. 85 (1983).

[216] *Shaw*, 463 U.S. at 97.

[217] *Ingersoll-Rand v. McClendon*, 498 U.S. 133, 139 (1990).

[218] 514 U.S. 645 (1995).

[219] *Id.* at 654.

[220] *Id.* at 655.

[221] *Id.* at 661.

[222] *De Buono v. NYSA-ILSA Medical and Clinical Services Fund*, 520 U.S. 806 (1997) (state tax on gross receipts of health care facilities not preempted by ERISA); *California Div. of Labor Standards Enforcement v. Dillingham Constr.*, 519 U.S. 316 (1997) (California's prevailing wage law not preempted by ERISA).

[223] *See* Constitution of the United States of America, Analysis and Interpretation, Congressional Research Service, p. 262, stating that ERISA's preemption provision is "[p]erhaps the broadest preemption section ever enacted."

[224] ERISA § 514(b)(2)(A), 29 U.S.C. § 1144(b)(2)(A).

[225] 538 U.S. 329 (2003).

[226] For many years, the Court, in evaluating whether a state law was saved from ERISA preemption under Section 514(b), examined, among other things, whether the state law in question regulated the "business of insurance" under the McCarran-Ferguson Act (an act describing federal and state roles in insurance regulation). *See, e.g., Metropolitan Life Insurance v. Massachusetts*, 471 U.S. 724 (1985); *Pilot Life v. Dedeaux*, 481 U.S. 41 (1987). Under the McCarran-Ferguson factors, a state law regulates the business of insurance if it (1) has the effect of transferring or spreading the policyholder's risk, (2) is an integral part of the policy relationship between the insurer and the insured, and (3) is limited to entities within the insurance industry that could be included under the savings clause.

[227] *Id.* at 334, 338.

[228] *Id.* at 334 (*citing Rush Prudential HMO Inc. v. Moran*, 536 U.S. 355, 366 (2002)).

[229] *Miller*, 538 U.S. at 338. In its explanation, the Court gave an example of a law that would require insurance companies to pay their janitors twice the minimum wage. The Court stated that while this type of law would be a requirement to engage in the business of insurance, it would not "regulate insurance" within the meaning of the savings clause. *See id.*

[230] *Id.*

[231] *Id.*

[232] *Id.* at 338-39.

[233] ERISA § 514(b)(2)(B), 29 U.S.C. § 1144.

[234] "Subrogation" can be defined as "the principle under which an insurer that has paid a loss under an insurance policy is entitled to all the rights and remedies belonging to the insured against a third party with respect to any loss covered by the policy." BLACK'S LAW DICTIONARY 1440 (7th ed. 1999). In other words, a subrogation provision could require a health plan participant to reimburse the plan for medical costs that the plan had paid, if the member recovers on a claim in a liability action against a third party.

[235] A self-funded (or self-insured) health plan is an employee benefit plan under which an employer provides health benefits directly to plan participants, as opposed to offering benefits through health insurance. Because self-funded plans do not provide benefits though insurance, they cannot be regulated by the states under the exemption to preemption provided by the savings clause.

[236] 498 U.S. 52 at 60-61 (*citing Metropolitan Life Ins. Co. v. Massachusetts*, 471 U.S. at 740-741).

[237] *See Metro. Life Ins. Co. v. Taylor*, 481 U.S. 58, 66 (1987).

[238] Health plans, life insurance plans, and plans that provide dependent care assistance, educational assistance, or legal assistance can be deemed "employee welfare benefit plans." under ERISA. See 29 U.S.C. § 1002(1).

[239] *See generally* EMPLOYEE BENEFITS LAW 355 (Matthew Bender 2d ed.) (2000).

[240] P.L. 99-272, tit. X, 100 Stat. 327 (1985). For additional information on COBRA, see CRS Report RL30626, *Health Insurance Continuation Coverage Under COBRA*, by Heidi G. Yacker.

[241] A "qualified beneficiary" can be an employee (who loses health coverage due to termination of employment or a reduction in hours), as well as a spouse or the dependent child of the employee. 29 U.S.C. § 1167.

[242] 29 U.S.C. § 1163.

[243] 29 U.S.C. § 1162(2).

[244] *See* 29 U.S.C. § 1 162(2)(A)(iv). For example, in the case of a death of a covered employee (a qualifying event under Section 603(1) of ERISA) coverage can be up to 36 months.

[245] P.L. 104-191, 110 Stat. 1936 (1996). For additional information on HIPAA, see CRS Report RL3 1634, *The Health Insurance Portability and Accountability Act (HIPAA) of 1996: Overview and Guidance on Frequently Asked Questions*, by Hinda Chaikind, Jean Hearne, Bob Lyke, and Stephen Redhead.

[246] A health insurance issuer is defined by ERISA as "an insurance company, insurance service, or insurance organization (including a health maintenance organization) which is licensed to engage in the business of insurance in the State...." 29 U.S.C. § 1191b.

[247] Group health plans and health insurance issuers that provide health coverage will be referred to collectively hereinafter as "health plans."

[248] 29 U.S.C. § 1181(a)(1)-(3).

[249] 29 U.S.C § 1181(d).

[250] "Creditable coverage" as defined under ERISA Section 701(c)(1) (29 U.S.C. § 1181 (c)(1)) includes coverage under a group health plan, health insurance, and various other means of health benefit coverage.

[251] 29 U.S.C. § 1182(a)(1)(A)-(H).

[252] 29 U.S.C. § 1182(b)(1).
[253] 29 U.S.C. § 1183.
[254] P.L. 104-204, tit.VII, 110 Stat. 2874 (1996).
[255] 29 U.S.C. § 1185a(a)(4).
[256] *See, e.g.*, H.R. 3997 (Engrossed Amendment as Agreed to by Senate) 110th Cong., 1st Sess. (2007). See also H.Res. 884 (As passed by the House) 110th Cong., 1st Sess. (2007).
[257] P.L. 104-204, tit. VI, 110 Stat. 2935 (1996).
[258] 29 U.S.C. § 1185(a)(1)(A)(I).
[259] 29 U.S.C. § 1185(a)(1)(A)(ii).
[260] P.L. 105-277, 112 Stat. 2681 (1998).
[261] 29 U.S.C. § 1185b.
[262] The *Taxpayer Relief Act of 1997* (P.L. 105-34) exempted state and local government plans from the nondiscrimination, minimum coverage, and minimum participation rules applicable to qualified plans.
[263] 26 U.S.C. § 401(a)(17).
[264] 26 U.S.C. § 415(b).
[265] 26 U.S.C. § 4980.
[266] 26 U.S.C. § 4980(d). The replacement plan can be either a DB plan or a DC plan.
[267] §§12011 and 12012 of P.L. 101-508. ERISA § 408(b), 29 U.S.C. § 1108(b).
[268] §801 of the PPA.
[269] 26 U.S.C. § 415(c)(1)(A).
[270] 26 U.S.C. § 402(g)(1).
[271] P.L. 107-16, 115 Stat. 38 (June 7, 2001).
[272] Both DB plans and DC plans are subject to the IRC nondiscrimination test.
[273] 26 U.S.C. § 414(q).
[274] For the purposes of the latter test, the average contribution percentage is defined as all employer contributions divided by total compensation. A third test — that at least 70% of NHCEs must be covered by the plan — will automatically satisfy the first test listed above.
[275] P.L. 99-5 14, 100 Stat. 2085 (Oct. 22, 1986).
[276] ERISA § 206(a), 29 U.S.C. § 1056(a); 26 U.S.C. § 401(a)(14).
[277] 26 U.S.C. §401(a)(9). Prior to the *Small Business Job Protection Act of 1996* distributions had to begin at age 70½, whether or not the participant had retired or separated from service.
[278] ERISA §3(2), 29 U.S.C. § 1002(2), as amended by §905 of the PPA.
[279] Distributions from a traditional IRA must begin by this date even if the individual is still working. There are no required distributions from a Roth IRA. 26 U.S.C. § § 408 and 408A.
[280] 26 U.S.C. §72(p).
[281] 26 U.S.C. § 72(t).
[282] The individual is not prohibited from being employed, or even from returning to work for the same employer, but there must be a period of separation that began after age 55.
[283] For these estimates, a low-wage worker is defined as one who earned 45% of the national average wage every year and a high-wage earner is defined as one who earned the maximum amount taxable under Social Security every year.
[284] 26 U.S.C. § 401(a)(5).
[285] 26 U.S.C. § 416. Small pension plans are most likely to fall into the top-heavy category.
[286] ERISA Section 3001 *et. seq.*, 29 U.S.C. § 1201 *et. seq.*
[287] ERISA Section 3002 *et. seq.*, 29 U.S.C. § 1202 *et. seq.*
[288] See section I(I) which discusses prohibited transactions under ERISA.
[289] ERISA Section 3003 *et. seq.*, 29 U.S.C. § 1203 *et. seq.*
[290] ERISA Section 3004, 29 U.S.C. § 1204 *et. seq.* Whether provisions of ERISA relate to the same subject matter under Section 3004 is determined by the Secretaries of Labor and the Treasury.
[291] Other requirements are provided under Title III. *See* ERISA Section 3001 *et. seq.*, 29 U.S.C. § 1201 *et. seq.*

[292] P.L. 109-171, 120 Stat. 4 (Feb. 8, 2006).
[293] ERISA § 4022, 29 U.S.C. § 1322.
[294] For example, for plans terminated in 2008, the maximum yearly guarantee for someone who retires at age 62 is $40,882; for someone who retires at age 55 it is $23,287. The maximum PBGC guaranteed benefit is not reduced for participants who elect early retirement with a disability that meets the standards for Social Security disability benefits.
[295] ERISA §§ 4041-4048; 29 U.S.C. §§ 1341-1348.
[296] ERISA §§ 4061-4071; 29 U.S.C. §§ 1361-1371.
[297] Section 506 of the PPA, amending ERISA § 4041.
[298] ERISA § 4006; 29 U.S.C. § 1306.
[299] ERISA §§ 4201-4225; 29 U.S.C. §§ 1381-1405.

Chapter Sources

The following chapters have been previously published:

Chapter 1 – This is an edited, excerpted and augmented edition of a United States Congressional Research Service publication, Report Order Code RS22827, dated March 4, 2008.

Chapter 2 – This is an edited, excerpted and augmented edition of a United States Congressional Research Service publication, Report Order Code RS22643, dated January 29, 2009.

Chapter 3 – This is an edited, excerpted and augmented edition of a United States Congressional Research Service publication, Report Order Code RL34443, dated April 10, 2008.

INDEX

O

P

Q

R

S

T

U

V

W